Understanding Cryptocurrencies

Understanding Cryptocurrencies

Bitcoin, Ethereum, and Altcoins as an Asset Class

Ariel Santos-Alborna

BEP

BUSINESS EXPERT PRESS

Leader in applied, concise business books

Understanding Cryptocurrencies:
Bitcoin, Ethereum, and Altcoins as an Asset Class

Copyright © Business Expert Press, LLC, 2022.

Cover design by Charlene Kronstedt

Interior design by Exeter Premedia Services Private Ltd., Chennai, India

First published in 2021 by
Business Expert Press, LLC
222 East 46th Street, New York, NY 10017
www.businessexpertpress.com

ISBN-13: 978-1-63742-099-7 (paperback)
ISBN-13: 978-1-63742-100-0 (e-book)

Business Expert Press Finance and Financial Management Collection

Collection ISSN: 2331-0049 (print)
Collection ISSN: 2331-0057 (electronic)

First edition: 2021

10 9 8 7 6 5 4 3 2 1

Description

Understanding Cryptocurrencies is perfect for both introductory investors to the digital asset space and experienced investors seeking to gain practical insight into frameworks for understanding digital assets and valuation metrics. The book provides in-depth analysis of Bitcoin, Ethereum, and the different types of Altcoins in the ecosystem. The author demonstrates an empirical approach to explaining how digital assets can fit into a diversified portfolio of traditional financial assets, or as a standalone portfolio in a parallel financial ecosystem. The book contains fundamental, technical, and on-chain analytic tools for investors to better understand Bitcoin price cycles that will ultimately lead to better returns. The capital from these price cycles oftentimes migrates to other digital assets, creating a robust ecosystem and providing opportunities for enterprising investors to generate additional alpha. In *Understanding Cryptocurrencies*, the author also offers options for asset custody and counterargument breakdowns to create better informed investors. Lastly, the author provides poignant insight into the economic inefficiencies created from decades of Central Bank interest rate manipulation and monetary expansion. These inefficiencies have had social, political, and economic implications. It is ultimately due to these inefficiencies that a global sound money vacuum exists for digital assets to exploit.

Keywords

bitcoin; ethereum; altcoins; digital assets; cryptocurrencies; blockchain; decentralized finance; scarcity; gold; stock-to-flow; transactions; payment; money; store of value; medium of exchange; utility; mayer multiple; market capitalization; real capitalization; bitcoin mining; miner capitulation; hash rate; hash ribbon; difficulty adjustment; diversification; portfolio management; technology; central bank; liquidity; interest rates; debt; growth; value; liquidity waterfall; risk curve; volatility; digital scarcity; price cycles

Contents

Introduction

This book answers two simple questions: what is Bitcoin and why should I invest in it? One of the most frequent complaints of Bitcoin literature is its opacity and overinclusion of coding or other language that prevents it from resonating with the average investor. This book is simple in its construction and written in a manner that is accessible to the lay investor. My hope is that this book serves as a starting point for understanding digital assets from a portfolio management perspective. The primary source to understand any digital asset is its white paper. I begin with an explanation of Bitcoin, with a large portion of the information taken from the white paper of Satoshi Nakamoto, Bitcoin's pseudonymous founder. I also incorporate my own analysis of Bitcoin as a digital store of value and a technological breakthrough. At its core, Bitcoin is software applied to the problem of fiat money.

In Chapter 2, I explain why Bitcoin deserves allocation in every investor's portfolio—diversification and extremely high growth potential. The level of investment depends on the individual investor's risk tolerance and conviction. There exists an allocation percentage for skeptics, allocation that provides true diversification, and, for full believers, the route of adopting the Bitcoin network as your personal savings account or treasury asset. As a macroeconomic investor and writer, the third chapter explains how decades of interest rate manipulation and money printing coming to a head has created the perfect storm for the price of Bitcoin. The economic inefficiencies created by Central Bank monetary policy created a sound money vacuum that Bitcoin will exploit in the coming decades.

Experienced investors will likely consider Chapter 4 the most important. Here, I explain Bitcoin valuation metrics to include a more in depth look at the Stock-to-Flow model introduced in Chapter 1, the Mayer Multiple, explaining network effects through Metcalfe's Law, and much more. Traditional models of discounted cash flows or venture capital valuation models do not work with a monetary network. Examining scarcity dynamics and number of users on the network assist the investor in knowing whether the asset is currently over or undervalued. Bitcoin has programmed scarcity and programmed cyclicality with its four year halving cycle. This book also provides methods to determine Bitcoin's stage in a typical four year market cycle.

After explaining all the ways to invest in Bitcoin, from price exposure in a trust to cold storage, I examine counterarguments for Bitcoin's mass adoption as an alternative store of value and payment network. Some common arguments against Bitcoin include the likelihood of government bans, criminals using the network, quantum computing, China's role in Bitcoin mining, and a better coin coming into existence that overtakes it. Any potential investor should understand each counterargument and the risk, if any, it poses to the network. I spend a majority of the book on Bitcoin because it is undoubtedly the dominant digital asset, whose existence usually serves an on-ramp that supports the proliferation of other digital assets.

The final two chapters of the book address Ethereum and other digital assets. Calling every decentralized, blockchain-based token a cryptocurrency is a misnomer. Ethereum and most tokens were never created to challenge Bitcoin in the role of a decentralized store of value and medium of exchange. Ethereum and Altcoins complement Bitcoin to create a robust crypto-ecosystem; however, each token has its own value proposition. In the digital asset risk curve, Altcoins offer greater volatility for potentially greater returns, but contain existential risks that do not exist in the Bitcoin network. Investors can allocate capital based on the digital asset risk curve concept, though I provide readers with a warning that the risk curve may not always exist in its current form, and greater risk also comes with the responsibility of greater due diligence on behalf of the investor. Most Altcoins in existence are not worth the investor's time or money. Similar to actively managed equity portfolios underperforming a simple index, dollar cost averaging into Bitcoin is likely the superior method for most investors.

For newcomers in the space, this book serves as a meaningful guide to begin your journey as a digital asset investor. For current investors, this book introduces new concepts and frameworks that should increase your knowledge base. Like many, I began looking at Bitcoin much too late. For me, that was near its peak in 2017 when it showed every sign of a speculative mania. A value investor at heart, I took a second look at Bitcoin when that mania turned into panic and loathing just a few months later. Frequently writing about the economic inefficiencies created from Central Bank policy, what I discovered in Bitcoin astounded me. I first recommended Bitcoin to my subscribers on SeekingAlpha at $10,750 in mid-2019. I continued my buy recommendation as the price moved against me to $7,000 and eventually to $3,000 in the midst of the COVID-19 liquidity shock. I want to thank the investors who believed in my analysis and conviction that Bitcoin's unique qualities makes it both a nascent asset class and technological breakthrough. On January 2020, I called Bitcoin the "Biggest Opportunity of 2020." It is not the biggest opportunity of 2020, but the opportunity of a generation. I hope this book provides readers with the tools and knowledge to attain monetary freedom or in the very least protect their portfolio from a devaluation-based stimulus model that Central Banks are adopting. I must remind readers that this is not financial advice, and to conduct additional research before making any investment decision.

CHAPTER 1

What Is Bitcoin?

The millennial generation and later, as natives to the Internet, seem to register the utility of cryptocurrencies more than generations before them. As an inverse of this observation, older generations understand the utility of investing in and storing physical gold. The value of each investment derives first and foremost from its scarcity. In addition to scarcity, Bitcoin contains characteristics that liken it more to a payment network such as Visa and PayPal than a store of value asset. To add complexity, we now see borrowing and lending systems with Bitcoin collateral and the steady introduction of new regulations concerning its custody and classification. How do investors classify something with such unique and diverse qualities?

Although there is no straight answer, I offer a three-pronged solution to the question posed as the title of this chapter. First and foremost, Bitcoin is a decentralized payment network; or as Twitter CEO Jack Dorsey states, "the best manifestation" of a global currency native to the Internet.[1] Due to its programmed scarcity in the face of fiat currency supply inflation, it also serves as a store of value. Any asset whose price appreciation outpaces the devaluation rate of the currency used to measure it can be said to sufficiently store value. Bitcoin, therefore, is also savings technology that allows you to store liquid dollars in a scarce protocol to avoid the Federal Reserve's programmed 2 percent devaluation rate. Lastly, Bitcoin is software applied to the problem of money and can therefore be likened to a high-growth tech stock, though it cannot be valued as such.

Peer-to-Peer Cash

All online payments not on the Bitcoin network necessitate a trusted third party in the form of a bank or credit card company to process the transaction. These financial institutions verify these transactions and prevent fraud in a process that takes time and fees. The average cost for credit card processing is between 1.3 and 3.4 percent.[2] Bitcoin, and blockchain technology in general, is revolutionary in that its decentralized nature eliminates rent-seeking behavior from those standing in the middle of value transactions. Bankers, lawyers, supply chain managers, and human resource representatives are all examples of professionals that will all be affected by this technology, whether they realize it yet or not.

The biggest issue with digital money has historically been double spending. This is where a fraudster spends the same digital token with multiple merchants. A trusted third party mediates transactions to prevent double spending of funds, but Bitcoin uses a distributed ledger system that records and confirms all transactions on the blockchain. While coins with digital signatures provide proof of ownership, a verifiable distributed ledger prevents the double spending fraud problem. Transactions are final once published on the blockchain, hence the cash aspect. Risks of a hack where an attacker owns over half of the nodes (a 51 percent attack) was a risk early in Bitcoin, but becomes less possible as its market capitalization reaches trillions of dollars. The more the network grows, the more secure it becomes. In addition to its near impossibility, hacking the Bitcoin network would undoubtedly crash its price. From a game theory perspective, the incentive structure of the network strongly discourages anyone from attacking it. All cases of Bitcoin fraud or hacks were really just phishing scams where the victim willingly gave up their private keys or sent funds to a fraudster. One is more likely to have his or her card information hacked from a company's centralized database than from the Bitcoin network.

Lastly, traditional banking takes time in addition to incurring fees and third-party risk. While micropayments occur instantly, larger payments such as international wire transfers take between one and five business days to settle. It is faster to physically send large sums of cash via express mail than conduct digital transfers under the current system—a perplexing fact given the current state of technology caused by the fact that technology has never really challenged financial infrastructure. Bitcoin transactions occur instantly and the funds post in the several minutes it takes for blocks on the chain to approve the transaction. At its core, Bitcoin allows individuals to send value over the Internet without a bank or trusted third party. While technologically impressive, I admit that this itself does not serve as a large enough catalyst to create parabolic price action.

Bitcoin will not subvert the payments industry altogether anytime soon as the current system is not overly cumbersome. A rule of thumb is that adopting a new technology will usually require a 10× improvement on current technology. Most consumers are not likely to transfer their cash to the Bitcoin network to avoid time and fees because they do not regularly conduct large-scale, international wire transfers. However, understanding how scarcity dynamics in Bitcoin affects the price is the true selling point. Absolute scarcity versus an inflationary monetary system is undoubtedly a 10× improvement. The next section is likely the most important for understanding the current value proposition of Bitcoin.

Digital Gold

What drives value? The Austrian School of Economics contends that all things contain utility value, scarcity value, or a mixture thereof. The air we breathe has ultimate utility value in that we need it to survive; however, its abundance makes it worthless as a sold good. A market for air manifests itself once it becomes scarce. Take Delhi in India, the fifth worst polluted city in the world. Oxygen bars have popped up for customers to breathe pure air for 300 rupees, roughly 4 dollars, per 15 minutes.[3]

Gold is the quintessential scarce good. Roughly 190,000 tons of gold have been mined historically, while an average of 2,900 tons are introduced each year through mining. One will find slight differences in these figures depending on the source used. The stock of 190,000 divided by the annual flow of 2,900 gives gold a Stock-to-Flow (SF) ratio of 66. That is, in 66 years the current stock of gold will double. For comparison's sake, silver has an SF of 22, platinum of 1.1, and palladium of 0.4. The obvious correlation is that the higher the SF ratio, the higher the market price due to a scarcity premium. Gold has served as a store of value for over 5,000 years because it has a limited supply and limited flows. It is the harder asset, with an inflation rate of 1.5 percent that is excellent compared to fiat currencies historically. The British pound, for example, has lost 99.5 percent of its value since its inception in 1209. A 13th-century British family could store their wealth in gold and still provide value to their relatives centuries later.

The argument in this section is as follows: if scarcity drives value, and scarcity can be measured by the SF ratio, a higher SF ratio means higher value (or price). Gold's scarcity is unforgeable due to its chemical properties. Bitcoin's scarcity is unforgeable due to its code. Bitcoin serves as a technologically enabled, perfectly scarce good. Except for the time we spend on this planet, perfect scarcity does not exist in the physical world.

To understand Bitcoin's scarcity, we have to understand the mining process. A mining reward occurs roughly every 10 minutes, when a miner uses electricity and computational power to find the hash that satisfies a proof-of-work requirement. It is the equivalent to finding the solution to a complex puzzle. Instead of a gold mining operation with machinery and manpower, think warehouses filled with servers. The mining reward started with 50 Bitcoin and is halved every 210,000 blocks, or roughly four years. The mining reward at the time of this writing is 6.25 Bitcoin.

Price action tends to increase substantially following a halving event. Why? Because the incoming flow was cut in half, the SF ratio doubles. If demand remained the same and supply gets cut in half, price increases. If demand increases at the same time, which we have seen with Bitcoin's adoption by CashApp, PayPal, Square, MicroStrategy, and retailers such as Microsoft, Whole Foods, and Starbucks, the price goes parabolic. Taking behavioral economics into account, increased price action also creates attention that attracts a growing investor and user base.

Bitcoin's SF doubles every four years. Its current SF of 50 nears gold's ratio of 66. Following the next halving event in 2024, Bitcoin will become more scarce than gold. The market capitalization of gold is roughly 9 trillion dollars. If investors own gold due its premium as a scarce store of value in the face of inflation or uncertainty, and Bitcoin will be more scarce than gold, it is possible that Bitcoin steals market capitalization away from precious metals. If Bitcoin attained a market capitalization of $9 trillion, the price per coin would be $500,000. In 2140, there will be no more Bitcoin to mine as the stock reaches 21 million. That means that Bitcoin will become the only asset in existence to achieve absolute scarcity. With an SF ratio of infinity, it will be the only investable asset as scarce as the time you spend on this planet. Its demand will increase as investors take note of its utility as a cheaper payment mechanism and a scarcer and more liquid store of value compared to physical gold, real estate, fine art, and so on. Programmed, decreasing supply couples with steadily increasing demand in what Bitcoiners refer to as "number go up" technology. Institutional finance is slowly catching on to the scarcity value proposition. However, retail investors have an opportunity to front-run the incoming wave of institutional money as regulations slowly become solidified.

Software Solves Money

This section delves into monetary history as well as the theoretical question of what is money. To begin with, the properties of money include divisibility, durability, portability, scarcity, and recognizability (its authenticity can be verified). Historically, the free market decided on the most acceptable money or form of payment based on these characteristics. Gold coins filled this function beginning with the Lydians in 700 BCE. Gold's chemical properties make it durable and scarce. However, it lacked portability due to its weight and divisibility due to its requirement to be melted. Merchants would also have to confirm its recognizability with each purchase to avoid accepting gold alloyed with other metals. The divisibility problem led to the issuance of silver and copper coins as less scarce and therefore less valuable money. Meanwhile, paper money backed by gold, coupled with centralized gold custody at Central Banks, solved the portability problem.

Historically, governments entrusted with the custody of gold and issuance of currency have always violated that trust and funded wars or public deficits through issuing money in excess of their gold reserves. For governments, the alternatives to debasing the money supply include finding new forms of financing or simply limiting their expenditures. From 54 AD to 305 AD, the gold content of Roman coins was reduced by half.[4] Centuries later in a similar tale, European powers left the gold standard in 1914 to finance World War I, and like Rome, lost their status as global hegemon soon thereafter. The story of the United States' 1971 severance of gold for dollar convertibility is a tale as old as time.

The post-World War II Bretton Woods system pegged all currencies to the dollar while the dollar was pegged to gold. Up until 50 years ago, global economies agreed that gold is the best form of currency. As previously mentioned, in 1971, President Nixon severed the convertibility of paper notes into gold. Why? The United States had printed more money than they had gold reserves. In 1965, French President Charles de Gaulle sent the French Navy across the Atlantic to exchange France's dollar reserves for physical gold. When Germany attempted to do the same, Nixon ended convertibility. This was in fact a default on the currency. The United States did not have the gold reserves to keep true to its promise of convertibility. This action compromised the scarcity of money. With no check on spending, deficits ballooned and inflation continuously eroded the value of money in circulation.

We currently straddle between two incomplete forms of money. Gold is durable and scarce, but not portable, divisible, or an accepted form of payment. It is a great store of value due to scarcity, but not an accepted medium of exchange. To test this theory, try paying for your groceries in gold coins. Dollars, or fiat currencies in general, are the recognized medium of exchange but a terrible store of value due to the ability of governments to print money without consequence—and print they do. By January 2021, twenty-two percent of all U.S. dollars in circulation were printed the previous year. The Federal Reserve prints money in order to avoid a deflationary collapse with the current amount of debt in the system. It also targets a 2 percent annual inflation rate. An achieved 2 percent inflation rate will lead to $1 becoming $2.59 in as little as 50 years. Chapter 3 will delve into why inflation targeting exists and why the present and future must involve more money printing than generations past. This inflation does not manifest itself equally among all goods and services. However, newly created paper money has no value. Instead, it takes value from the currency in circulation at the time, primarily hurting those with savings and fixed salaries.

Bitcoin is savings technology that solves the inflationary problem of fiat money. The current system punishes workers by continuously debasing their wages and grants exorbitant privilege to the government, banks, and corporations allowed to borrow at low or negative real rates. It rewards large debtors. Think of the interest rate as the cost of borrowing. The real interest rate is the nominal interest rate minus inflation. For example, if you took out a personal loan with no collateral at 9 percent interest, which is quite typical for the average borrower, a 2 percent inflation rate means your real rate is 7 percent. The biggest debtors of all are the U.S. government and large corporations. The U.S. government issues bonds to spend money it currently does not have and pays interest to the bondholder. The current rate on a 10-year treasury note is 0.93 percent. With a 2 percent target inflation rate, the real rate becomes 0.92 − 2= −1.07. That's correct, inflation allows the government to continue its debt-based growth and spending patterns. In fact, they receive a premium when they issue debt. In Europe and Japan, the epitome of monetary policy run amuck, governments issue negative yielding bonds. The interest rate on AT&T's 10-year corporate bond is 1.9 percent at the time of this writing, meaning AT&T and similar indebted corporations can also issue money for free. The toxic combination of low borrowing costs and inflation is essentially a tax on savers and employees with fixed wages to fund U.S. government and corporate spending.

Nominal yields may not remain at such subdued levels under conditions of a robust recovery or rising inflation fears. Additionally, the Federal Reserve does not directly dictate corporate bond yields. However, loose credit conditions set by the Fed reverberate through capital markets in their entirety. A policy set by the Federal Reserve of below free market level interest rates and above free market level inflation incentivizes the aforementioned dynamic of cheaply raising capital through debt issuances.

This system also rewards asset owners. Why would the price of stocks and real estate reach all-time highs in the middle of a pandemic, where millions of Americans cannot pay rent and small business are forced to close with a lack of cash flow? For one, the financial system needs inflation if it has any chance to service the debt and prevent a deflationary collapse brought about by higher debt service costs. It also needs appreciating asset prices because U.S. equity market capitalization is 160 percent of Gross Domestic Product and 200 percent of annual personal consumption expenditures derive from a combination of capital gains and taxable Individual Retirement Account distributions.[5] Luke Gromen, Founder and President of the research provider Forest for the Trees, aptly states that in the United States, the stock market *is* the economy. If 65 percent of U.S. GDP is consumption, and consumption is inextricably linked to capital gains from a growing stock market, the Fed cannot afford for stock prices to go down without creating a recession in the real economy. Furthermore, the mechanism by which newly created money enters the economy means that it stays within the financial system and fuels asset appreciation first. A system that lifts asset prices while suppressing wages results in an ever-expanding wealth gap. Putting your savings in a scarce and liquid store of value allows you to opt out of the implicit savings tax imposed by economic central planners. That is why Bitcoin solves money.

Bitcoin also solves the exchangeability problem of physical gold. The list of merchants accepting it grows every year. Even if some major merchants never accept Bitcoin as a medium of exchange, its digital nature allows for a seamless transition to U.S. dollars, dollar-backed stablecoins, or whichever fiat currency the consumer needs. Contrast this to taking physical gold coins to a gold buyer in your local city or town, and one can see the benefits of digitization. Technological breakthroughs oftentimes solve a problem we did not know existed. With Amazon, we do not need to rely on physical retail locations to make purchases. With Google, we do not need to rely on books or encyclopedias to obtain information. With Apple iPhones, we do not need to rely on one device for calls and texts, one device for e-mails, and one device for music. With Bitcoin we do not need to rely on a dollar that will continually devalue as a matter of policy. Investors have a perfectly liquid market to store their dollars for future use. Though they currently have to convert it back to dollars for most transactions, this may not always be the case.

Conclusion

As readers can tell, the answer to the question posed at the beginning of the chapter is not a straightforward one. Bitcoin has qualities that liken it to a payment network, digital gold, and high-growth technology companies providing a valuable service. These qualities put together make it a valuable asset to have in the portfolio. As Chapter 4 will explore, we can use certain models to assign a numerical value. Bitcoin's value proposition makes it an alternative asset whose rightful place belongs with gold, real estate, collectible art, technology stocks, and venture capital. It connects the age-old concepts of scarce money with 21st-century concepts of breakthrough technology. Once we see it as an asset worthy of our investment, the question arises as to how much to allocate. Again, the answer is nuanced and depends on an investor's conviction and risk profile.

CHAPTER 2

How Bitcoin Fits in Your Portfolio

Enemy analysis plays an important role in mission planning in the armed forces. We examine composition, to include number of enemy personnel by weapon type and take note of the max effective range of each enemy weapon. We examine disposition, which is how the enemy arrays itself on the battlefield and how they generally fight. We examine strength, simply a percentage of their fully manned composition. We also examine and brief two potential futures—the most likely course of action and the most deadly course of action.

In truth, investing is not much different from studying and fighting an enemy force. The planner first gathers and examines all available information. He or she determines the most likely outcome of future events based on that information, and allocates capital or creates a plan depending on the mission and information given. In investing, that mission is always to preserve and grow your capital. The Platoon Leader and his or her subordinate leaders execute the plan but have a contingency if the most deadly course of action manifests itself, even if that contingency constitutes a simple break contact. In investing, this is our stop loss. The leader incorporates as many forms of contact as possible. This includes direct fire from rifles or machine guns, indirect fire from artillery or mortars, obstacles to block or canalize a force, electronic warfare to jam communications systems, even air support or chemical if the rules of engagement allows it. This is diversification. Relying on a single form of contact is simply too risky.

Just as with mission planning, I would like to lay out to the reader the most probable outcome and most dangerous outcome with Bitcoin's future. The most probable outcome is that Bitcoin becomes an alternative investment class and several sovereignty minded individuals, corporations, and nation-states choose to adopt it as their reserve asset. It incrementally takes market cap from gold seeing as it better performs the functions of gold and has a small part as an alternative asset in nearly every retail, hedge fund, and pension portfolio. Outside of the investment management space, an increasing number of corporations and sovereign nations hold Bitcoin as a reserve asset. Though many retailers may accept it, Bitcoin never truly displaces fiat currency as the dominant medium of exchange because tax regimes vary from state to state. The Bitcoin max- imalist proposition states that hard money will eventually drive out fiat money in what is known as Thier's Law, the inverse of Gresham's Law. Free market actors will converge on Bitcoin as a superior form of money, and governments everywhere will be forced to adopt the Bitcoin Standard.

In terms of institutional adoption, hedge fund titans Paul Tudor Jones and Stan Druckenmiller have already gone public saying they invest in Bitcoin. The Massachusetts insurance giant MassMutual purchased $100 million Bitcoin for its investment account in late 2020. CashApp, PayPal, and Square have moved to accepting Bitcoin payments. The National Football League's Russell Okung opted to receive half his salary in Bitcoin and had the request approved. El Salvador also declared Bitcoin as legal tender in 2021. My base case is that this trend continues into the future. These are the first movers whose decision most will see as overtly risky but will pay off immensely as adoption rates increase.

Ironically, the latecomer to this party thus far has been Wall Street. Goldman Sachs published a report in May 2020 that likened Bitcoin to the Dutch tulip mania of the 17th century and labeled it a "conduit for illicit activity."[1] Goldman Sachs reached a $3.9 billion settlement that same year for admitted money laundering with the 1Maylasia Devel- opment Berhad.[2] Additionally, Bitcoin received legal status an asset by the Commodity Futures Trading Commission in 2015. Many major banks such as Chase, Wells Fargo, and Bank of America also prohibit Bitcoin purchases using their debit or credit accounts. Wall Street and conventional banking's reluctance to accept Bitcoin makes intuitive sense. Bitcoin's peer-to-peer nature disrupts the hierarchical, fee and inter- est-based models of conventional banking. However, their initial hostility is slowly fading as the opportunity to generate profit in the space becomes clear. The banks can either become involved in the space or become less relevant. I believe they are choosing the latter as evidenced by J.P. Morgan Chase and Goldman Sachs appointing new heads of digital assets strategy in 2020 and creating custody solutions. Additionally, after years of lambasting the best performing asset of the decade to ultrawealthy private clients, wealth management divisions of these megabanks risk losing a large source of income if they ignore the transformation to digital assets and growing ecosystem. Recent trends indicate they recognize this.

Again, my base case is that Bitcoin becomes a highly sought-after asset due to its unique qualities as a scarce and liquid store of value, arriving at a $9 trillion market capitalization, on par with gold, for $500,000 a coin within the next decade. Much of the world adopting the Bitcoin Standard constitutes a positive tail risk event. Though most countries will not willingly give up the privilege of seigniorage, others are highly incentivized to adopt Bitcoin as a currency or reserve asset. These include countries such as El Salvador that use the dollar as their primary medium of exchange and have their monetary policy imposed upon them by unelected officials in the United States, or countries seeking to escape the rat race of constant competitive devaluation that is the inevitable byproduct of a floating exchange rate system. A globally coordinated ban of Bitcoin constitutes a negative tail risk event with low likelihood of occurring due to its difficulty to achieve. For readers who believe that Bitcoin could never displace gold as the go-to global store of value, I remind them that Bitcoin solves the liquidity and physical storage issues of gold with a programmed higher stock-to-flow ratio. Bitcoin is to gold what the car was to the horse and carriage. In a 1911 article in the *Saturday Evening Post*, Alexander Winton, whose Winton Motor Carriage Company sold the first automobile in 1897, wrote about his discouragement regarding global skepticism about the automobile. His banker told him, "You're crazy if you think this fool contraption you've been wasting your time on will ever displace the horse."[3] Motor vehicles were a 10× improvement on the horse and carriage in terms of speed and maintainability. Decades later, we know that history took sides with Mr. Winton.

Just as in tactics, we must examine the most dangerous course of action, which is that all G7 nations collude to ban Bitcoin. I include a more in-depth description of why this is unlikely in the counterarguments section later in the book. While most Bitcoin enthusiasts will claim that

Bitcoin can never be banned because it is open source code, governments colluding to make Bitcoin payments illegal or shut down exchanges will undoubtedly destroy the price. However, it must be all nations making it illegal and at the same time due to international arbitrage if banning occurs in a haphazard manner. For example, if one country made Bitcoin payments, storage, or mining illegal, those whose businesses depended on it would simply move to a country where it is legal. In fact, the country who made it illegal would be losing an entire industry while the open country would gain one. Using game theory, countries are better off accepting Bitcoin than banning it. A similar dynamic has already occurred with mining operations in China migrating to the United States, Kazakhstan, and Malaysia. International cooperation has always proven difficult and a different country would simply reap the benefits of a ban.

Additionally, I believe that institutional acceptance is too broad and only broadening for it to be made illegal. Hedge funds, corporations, investment banks, pension funds, insurance companies, and sovereign nations have all begun moving a small percentage of their assets to Bitcoin or have become involved in the space. Unless governments act now, outlawing it would create insolvencies in an already underfunded pension system. On the other side, the capital gains acquired from Bitcoin could actually save those pension systems that act as first movers. The incentives are heavily in favor of Bitcoin's adoption. The only seemingly negative proposed regulation for mass adoption is the government's rumored desire to increase regulation on self-hosted or cold storage wallets, which has already faced opposition from lawmakers. Cold storage involves keeping one's Bitcoin offline and off of exchanges in a hardware wallet, paper wallet, desktop wallet, or USB drive. It is the equivalent of owning your own physical gold away from the financial system. The reason cold storage makes the government wary is due to its intractability and the fear of terrorist financing. While certainly against the libertarian nature of early Bitcoin adopters, a ban on cold storage will not destroy Bitcoin. In fact, the news of Secretary Mnuchin's rumored ban in 2020 barely put a dent in Bitcoin's price and never came to fruition. Price action ignored the rumors as it moved to all-time highs.

Alternatively, I believe Central Banks and governments are moving more toward accepting Bitcoin than banning it. I will discuss Central

Global institutional adoption as store of value

Global collusion to
slow Bitcoin
adoption / niche
store of value

$\sigma = 1$

Central Bank
Reserve Asset

-1   0   1

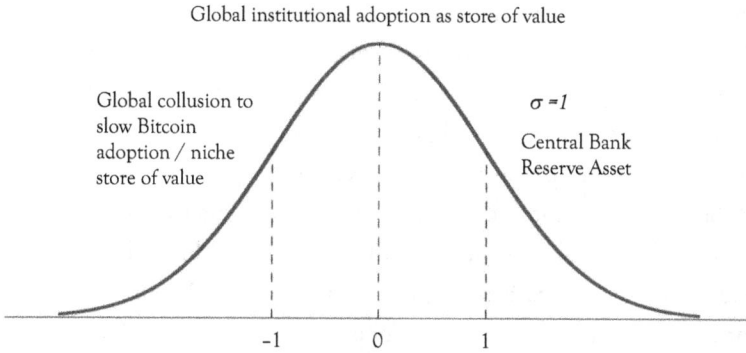

Figure 2.1 Normal distribution of bitcoin probabilities

Bank Digital Currencies (CBDCs) later in the book and how countries and central bankers have already expressed their desires to create them in order to provide more effective stimulus. Blockchain based, government-issued tokens provide easy on-ramps for would-be crypto investors. In other words, CBDCs will enable the transition from physical dollars and gold to digital dollars and Bitcoin. In a system of Bitcoin acting as an internationally recognized global reserve asset, the price per coin would be in the several millions.

A concerted international effort to ban Bitcoin and sovereign adoption are both tail risks in the distribution of probabilities as shown in Figure 2.1. However, the odds are heavily skewed in favor of continued price appreciation. The most likely scenario involves its institutional adoption as an alternative asset class. In this case, the asset will remain significantly undervalued for years. Now that we have examined the possible distribution of outcomes, the next sections explore the practical reasons to own Bitcoin.

Diversification and Risk

Diversification plays a vital role in portfolio construction and management. Ray Dalio, founder and chief investment officer of Bridgewater Associates, one of the largest hedge funds in existence with $138 billion assets under management, claims that "diversifying well is the most important thing you need to do in order to invest well."[4] His "Holy Grail" of diversification involves 15 uncorrelated bets. For one, how many investors can say they have even 10 uncorrelated bets? Additionally, as the next chapter suggests, false diversification is a true threat to portfolios as stocks, government bonds, and corporate bonds are all markets that see artificial demand from Fed policy and anticorrelation based on a Fed reaction function that has run its course.

Statistically, according to coinmetrics.io, Bitcoin's correlation with traditional assets such as the S&P 500, the dollar, gold, and volatility as measured by the VIX, has ranged from 0.22 to −0.21. Historically, the correlation remained closer to zero for each. The S&P correlation and VIX anticorrelation peaks both occurred in November 2020, as Bitcoin and U.S. equities rallied simultaneously and volatility decreased after March's COVID-19-related spike. I believe investors' risk appetite returned after the March shock and Fed response, causing both assets to rally simultaneously. However, a correlation range between 0.22 and −0.21 throughout its history tells investors that Bitcoin is not correlated to traditional assets. If investors know they should seek diversification, Bitcoin provides a solution as a statistically proven uncorrelated return stream.

In addition to diversification, Bitcoin also decreases risk in a portfolio as outlined in the article "Efficient Market Hypothesis and Bitcoin Stock-to-Flow Model."[5] The article presents the risk/return profile of traditional assets such as the S&P 500, government bonds, and gold. It defines risk as maximum historical annual loss and return as average annual returns. Bonds have the lowest of each, with the lowest risk of 8 percent but the lowest returns of 6 percent. Gold has a risk of 33 percent maximum loss and an average return of 7.5 percent. U.S. equites fell opposite to bonds with 40 percent risk of loss and 8 percent average return. How did Bitcoin fall on this metric? Two hundred percent average annual return and a maximum 80 percent loss. No other asset in existence provides even one-tenth of the alpha that Bitcoin has brought its investors. Bitcoin investors must know that it is a volatile asset but undoubtedly the best performing one due to the macroeconomic role that it plays. Since 2009, if you allocated 1 percent of your portfolio to Bitcoin and 99 percent to cash, you would achieve over 8 percent returns while only risking 1 percent of your capital. A 1 percent allocation to Bitcoin would have outperformed the S&P.

The Sharpe Ratio was developed by Nobel Prize winning economist William Sharpe. The equation takes the expected or historic rate of return, subtracts the risk-free rate of return (government bond yield matching the investment duration), and divides it by the volatility, or how widely prices disperse from their mean. It is seen as a measure of risk in traditional portfolio management. Personally, I believe most traditional portfolio managers conflate volatility with risk. For example, as the next chapter will explain, there is systemic risk to government bonds but their volatility is suppressed with Fed purchases. This leads to the false impression that bonds are not risky when in fact they are just not volatile. Nonetheless, using traditional financial logic, Bitcoin beats every other asset on this risk model.

A Sharpe Ratio of one is considered good and two is considered excellent, while a zero or negative Sharpe Ratio indicates that the asset will not outperform the risk-free rate. Since mid-2014, Bitcoin's Sharpe Ratio has never dipped below two and is currently at three. The S&P and gold are at roughly 1.3, while U.S. real estate is just below that at 1.1.[6] Using traditional measures of risk, Bitcoin is a superior and less risky investment than stocks, bonds, gold, and real estate at nearly double the Sharpe Ratio. Given Bitcoin's volatility, most investors could not stomach overallocation. However, adding Bitcoin to a traditional portfolio will optimize it by substantially increasing the risk-adjusted returns.

Bitcoin is an uncorrelated asset with a super risk/return profile. Adding it to your portfolio is akin to adding a proven venture capital arm to your investments. It does not correlate with traditional market movements unless in a liquidity event and its returns are astounding—even when compared to its volatility or existential risk. I believe that at some point, all portfolio managers and investment advisors will catch on to the fact that they can optimize their investments by adding even a small allocation to Bitcoin. If they already do, they are ahead of the game. If they do not, then much like some Wall Street banks, they will be forced to adopt by their clients or be forced into irrelevancy.

High Growth Potential and Network Effects

Bitcoin is a hard money monetary network. Facebook is a social media network. The telephone operates on a voice communications network. What matters to a network is the number of users. The features of

Facebook mean nothing if there are no other users on the platform to share and connect with, just as owning a telephone means nothing if there is no one to communicate with. The incentive structure of Bitcoin is rather straightforward. As it attracts more users to adopt the network as a store of value for their savings or as a payment mechanism to avoid time and fees involved with traditional banking, the price appreciates.

Metcalfe's Law, named after Internet pioneer Robert Metcalfe, explains how growth in networks differ from growth in typical businesses. Metcalfe's Law states that the value of a network increases by the square of the number of nodes or users. While a typical business increases linearly depending on the number of users, networks increase exponentially. In a typical business, each customer interacts with the business owner on an individual basis to conduct a transaction. In a network, each user becomes connected to each other user in the network, which in turn increases value for all users. This law quantifies the network effect.

Each user makes the network more robust and provides a node that all users can exchange value with on the network. Metcalfe's Law explains the parabolic growth rate of Google, Facebook, and Amazon as dominant networks in their fields. If each additional user increases the price exponentially, and institutional finance is just now joining the network in a large way, Bitcoin has astounding growth potential. If Bitcoin becomes the dominant store of value network, equaling or surpassing gold in market capitalization, the price per coin will be $500,000 per coin or greater. I believe that this is the realm that Bitcoin will eventually be relegated to—the monetary network that solved the gold/dollar dilemma. However, it has the potential to become much more.

Nothing Else Makes Sense

In this section, I will take the reader around the world of traditional asset classes to explain why, on a valuation basis, nearly every other asset cannot provide the same returns as Bitcoin. Investors need to take a value-minded framework yet understand technology and nuance in order to avoid being stuck in a 1970s-style stock picking mental model that will undoubtedly lead to lower returns. Bitcoin is undervalued not on a discounted cash flow basis but based on the network effects of the adoption curve.

U.S. Stocks

The post-2008 stock market is liquidity driven, not fundamentals driven. Barring a deflationary shock, equities will remain objectively overvalued because policy makers need stocks to rise to prevent a stock market recession from reverberating into the real economy. The following is a list of six common S&P 500 valuation metrics and their historical percentile only eight months after the coronavirus-created recession:[7]

1. U.S. Market Cap to GDP: 100 percent
2. Price to Sales: 100 percent
3. Price to Book: 100 percent
4. Enterprise Value to EBITDA: 100 percent
5. Price to Earnings: 98 percent
6. Cyclically Adjusted Price to Earnings (CAPE): 97 percent

This stock market is the most expensive in history by nearly every measure at a time where every large sell-off is quickly backstopped by the Fed. If future returns are a function of the price paid, the above metrics scream stay away from U.S. stocks. As the first sentence of this section suggests, I have a more nuanced view on the U.S. stock market. While they are objectively at nosebleed levels, they are only slightly overvalued on a liquidity basis. My advice to subscribers at Seeking Alpha is to remain cautiously long. Equity prices have a high correlation to global liquidity. Ratios such as asset prices to global liquidity and equity to safe assets matter more than the value investor metrics of decades ago. As a relatively scarce claim on a company's cash flows and growth, stocks act as a buffer against an inflating money supply. Demonstrating the importance of available liquidity, the Venezuelan stock market has returned 2,578 percent from January 2020 to March 2021. On a fundamental basis, nothing occurring in Venezuela would warrant such an increase besides a hyperinflating currency. The second metric, the equity to safe haven ratio, displays the level of widespread investor participation compared to treasuries and gold. A large percentage of investors positioning themselves defensively indicates that markets have not reached bubble territory. If equities should continue to rally, it will be on a liquidity basis.

Many renowned value investors will argue that fundamentals must converge onto inflated asset prices through the wealth effect or asset prices must converge onto weaker fundamentals through a sustained recession. These investors, including Warren Buffett, will patiently and confoundedly sit on mountains of cash waiting for opportunities to arise that seem to never materialize. They are right to note the disconnect between value and fundamentals. Apple's stock gained 92 percent in 2020 despite only increasing revenue by 1 percent. However, I will take readers back to my previous comment about understanding nuance and outdated mental models. The stock market is not the economy—even though economic activity has previously proven a successful barometer of present and future stock prices. We have unprecedented Central Bank activity aimed at preventing asset price collapse. As the system currently stands, tell me the direction of the Fed balance sheet and I will tell you the direction of U.S. equities.

The next chapter will take a closer look at why this disconnect occurs through the Cantillon Effect. In essence, the mechanism by which the Fed infuses the economy with liquidity leads to asset price inflation. In addition to this, velocity of money stops at banks as that money rarely makes it to the real economy. As previously mentioned, the system inadvertently takes money from savers and wage earners to boost asset prices. For the sake of this chapter, readers must know that newly created money most frequently goes to stocks before the real economy. Therefore, investors who allocate capital based on a framework of fundamental valuation will not do well in this environment. I do not recommend putting 100 percent of one's capital into equities. While they may have more upside on a liquidity basis, the only thing propping up equity markets is Central Bank liquidity.

Because financial markets are a complex system, I usually refrain from making normative statements. However, some relations are obvious. Anyone who makes a fundamental argument for stocks based on future earnings or valuation metrics will have a difficult time explaining equity prices when priced in things other than the dollar. Divide the U.S. stock market capitalization by G4 Central Bank liquidity and the stock market peaked in 2007 as quantitative easing began in earnest following the Global Financial Crisis. Divide the stock market capitalization by a hard asset such as gold and the stock market peaked in 2001. Divide it by a harder asset in Bitcoin and the stock market breaks down completely.

Quantitative easing went into hyperdrive following the coronavirus recession. In March of 2020 alone, global Central Banks purchased $1.4 trillion worth of assets. It is important to not examine equities through a silo. In terms of price, stocks always seem to go up. In terms of hard money, they have gone nowhere at all.

Investors overallocated to U.S. stocks should feel uneasy knowing that the only thing preventing prices from mean reversion is artificial demand from a cash infusion mechanism that benefits financial assets over real economic activity. Hard assets benefit even more from this monetary creation and should therefore play a larger role in future portfolios. This regime of high-powered monetary creation will not end in the foreseeable future.

Government and Corporate Bonds

Buying the 10-year Treasury note at near-zero rates a bet that yields will go zero or negative. When investors purchase a bond fund, the fund appreciates in price as yields decrease. That is because the fund rolls over its bonds, the equivalent of refinancing, and takes advantage of the gains acquired from the lower rate. Based on this dynamic, both government and corporate bond prices have remained on a steady uptrend for the past 40 years as the Federal Reserve forced interest rates lower and lower. If widespread inflation occurs, selling will force yields to rise. This constitutes an enormous risk amidst the current level of money printing. Similar to the Reserve Bank of Australia, the Fed will likely resort to yield curve control to prevent rising yields from pricking bubbles in the financial and real economy.

Buying bonds is the equivalent of picking up pennies in front of a steamroller. For long-term investors, I do not recommend them. For tactical traders, yields may eventually go to zero or even negative as they have in Europe and Japan. However, the gains acquired from a bond position when yields go negative is likely not worth the pain that will result if persistent inflation arises. The reason Europe and Japan have negative rates is simple. They need negative real yields to service their massive amount of debt and continue deficit spending. If real yields are equal to nominal yields minus the inflation rate, and the inflation rate in those countries are at zero or negative due to terrible demographics, low growth, and technological advances, nominal yields must be negative to keep real yields negative. These countries are victims of their own poor choices in economic governance. Japan did it first, Europe followed, and the United States is on a crash course to negative yields unless they change course. The only thing that will force the United States to change course is inflation brought about by poor policy choices. I believe the United States has implicitly stated it will inflate the debt away—a boon for Bitcoin and a death knell for bonds. Trillions of dollars in the bond market will need to find a new home in this paradigm shift from debt-based growth to inflation-based growth. Bitcoin will certainly be one of those homes. While bond prices may appreciate in the interim, better opportunities for generating alpha exist.

Government and corporate bonds have historically played an integral role in portfolio management due to their anticorrelation with equities. Investors purchase bonds to protect their portfolio in case of a large sell-off in equities. However, bonds moved opposite of stocks because the Federal Reserve pushed interest rates lower in the face of weaker economic activity as a counter to the business cycle. They were able to do this because there was no inflation risk as measured by a low Consumer Price Index. This is a modern phenomenon that began with the end of the inflationary regime of the 1970s and the beginning of accommodative monetary policy in the Greenspan era. Since 1883, stocks and bonds have had a highly positive correlation 30 percent of the time and a highly negative correlation 11 percent of the time. In a world where much of the financial system is leveraged to a 60/40 portfolio based on an assumption of anticorrelation, negative returns in both assets will devastate most portfolios and expose a gigantic recency bias.[8] While correlations may swing wildly, stocks do not always move opposite bonds. In fact, for most of history they moved in lockstep. Stocks, government bonds, and corporate bonds all benefit from Fed policy and have reached historical highs because of it. If they are destined to underperform due to their current valuations, what other assets exist?

Gold

Gold is seen as a safe haven asset and inflation hedge due to its scarcity value and its proven 5,000-year track record as a store of value. Some investors claim that gold and Bitcoin both play important roles in this macroeconomic environment of unprecedented money creation. However, I will take readers back to an argument made previously. If Bitcoin has perfected all of the characteristics that make gold valuable, why would investors still allocate to gold aside from an appeal to tradition bias? In fact, if paper currencies only came into existence to overcome the physical limitations of gold, and the technology exists to send digital gold via communications channels, there is theoretically no need for physical gold or paper currencies.

Nevertheless, with money being devalued at historic rates, a scarce store of value matters. A perfectly liquid and perfectly scarce store of value is preferable to an illiquid store of value with a near 2 percent inflation rate. Investors need to travel from point A to point B. Their options are a horse and buggy or an automobile. Both options allow them to achieve their goal but Bitcoin gets you there faster. Many investors see regulation risk as a legitimate reason to own some gold instead of Bitcoin. Though a reasonable objection, I believe much of that risk is overstated.

Real Estate

I am slightly more constructive on real estate than the previously mentioned asset classes. While prices generally are at historic highs due to decades of monetary debasement and low borrowing costs, pockets of value exist in real estate markets. Megacity real estate markets will have a brush with reality as ever-increasing house prices meets a millennial and Gen-Z generation entering the workforce after decades of stagnant wages and saddled with student debt. I do not recommend buying property or even Real Estate Investment Trusts (REITs) in mega-cities such as New York City or Los Angeles. However, in certain areas, an investor can pay a low price for a property that provides cash flow and has room to appreciate in price based on demand for that location.

Real estate can be profitable with a research-intensive and bargain-based approach. Prices should continue to rise with current rates of monetary debasement. However, real estate falls into the same category as U.S. equities in that I would be "cautiously long." Turning off the monetary spicket or substantially raising interest rates will hurt the real estate market. The notion that real estate prices always go up is simply a misunderstanding. House prices do not always go up, fiat always goes down.

Other Assets and Final Thoughts

From a value perspective, I am bullish on emerging market equities. I do not see the dollar losing reserve currency status in the near-term future but I see it as less dominant in the coming decades. Asia and Latin America constitute two areas with demographic tailwinds and a less significant debt burden to drag on future growth. With a weaker dollar and less dollar dominance in global trade, their dollar denominated debt burden will decrease, unlocking growth that rivals the post-World War II boom of the United States. Commodities are also beaten up from a valuation perspective and will benefit from both the economic reflation and monetary inflation narratives. Both assets have yet to outperform U.S. stocks. A strong dollar keeps debt burdens high for countries with dollar-based debt and slow economic activity prevents the industrial use of commodities. I believe these assets will see their decade in the sun but that time may be several years away.

Therefore, global assets fall into one of two categories. Stocks, bonds, and real estate are all at historical highs. They have limited upside and substantial downside. Gold is set to perform well but Bitcoin is theoretically superior to gold and has outperformed it by over 200 percent year over year. If one purchases gold and Bitcoin for the exact same reasons, yet Bitcoin outperforms by 200 percent, it questions the original thesis of why own both. Emerging markets and commodities are worthwhile future investments but will take time before the narrative catches on and their value is unlocked. Though I recommend diversification and several uncorrelated investment streams for most traditional investors, nothing else is set to perform like Bitcoin.

Conclusion

This chapter has outlined the reasons why investors should allocate some Bitcoin to their portfolio. It is an uncorrelated asset that provides true diversification. Using the Sharpe Ratio, it optimizes the risk-free returns of any portfolio. It has high growth potential due to network effects and continued adoption from institutional finance. Lastly, every other asset class is either severely overvalued or has not seen the flows to appreciate in price despite a bullish narrative.

Given these facts, how much should an investor allocate to Bitcoin? I offer three options depending on one's conviction. For skeptical investors, I hope the chapter on Bitcoin counterarguments will eliminate or reduce skepticism. However, I recommend a 1 to 5 percent allocation simply for portfolio optimization purposes. Another way to think about it is to invest whatever you are willing to lose. Past performance shows that even a 1 percent allocation to Bitcoin and 99 percent cash would have outperformed the S&P 500 since 2009. For those that desire true diversification, I recommend 10 to 15 percent. This allows you to gain from the massive appreciation I see coming with the macroeconomic tailwinds and have enough outside exposure to survive dreaded crypto bear markets—even though Chapter 4 will go over ways to know it is time to reduce exposure. The final option is not necessarily a percentage of one's investable assets but more of a lifestyle change. It involves adopting the Bitcoin Standard in one's personal life. Money intended for future consumption gets placed on the Bitcoin network. It serves as the hard money savings account that inflationary policy never let you have.

Michael Saylor is the Founder and CEO of MicroStrategy, a business analytics software company. He has garnered massive attention for his business decision to place over half of his company's cash holdings in Bitcoin. In essence, Bitcoin is his treasury reserve asset instead of the dollar. This is what I mean by adopting Bitcoin as a savings technology in one's personal life or business. If savings will be losing value daily and no worthwhile investments exist, simply place that savings in a hard money monetary network until the time comes to make a purchase. Thus far, companies such as Microstrategy, Square, and Tesla have been rewarded by the market with stock price appreciation for their business decision to place some cash reserves in Bitcoin.

I believe my journey is a typical one for investors. I allocated 5 percent to Bitcoin as an interested skeptic in 2018. As opposed to rebalancing in the face of price appreciation, I continued my research and grew in conviction. Once an investor has skin in the game, his or her perspective on money and portfolio management will change. My one recommendation involves starting small and getting off zero. The desire for diversification and greater risk adjusted returns may even morph into a *modus operandi* after investors realize that no other asset makes quite as much sense.

CHAPTER 3

Macroeconomics, Monetary Policy, and Bitcoin's Perfect Storm

In November 1989, Mexico City began implementing its "Hoy no circula" driving program, translating to "today, [your car] does not circulate." This was a government policy designed to reduce city pollution by reducing the number of cars on the road by day. The last number on your license plate dictated whether or not you could drive that day. Two numbers per day, from 5 a.m. to 10 p.m., were banned from driving. The Mexican government wanted an increased reliance on public transportation and ridesharing to cut down on city pollution. What they got was families buying second or third cars to avoid the new restrictions. Oftentimes they purchased old, inefficient cars seeing as they would only use the vehicle once or twice per week. The number of motor vehicles in Mexico more than tripled from 1990 to 2019 and carbon emission levels rose 13 percent.[1]

This is the law of unintended consequences. Politicians with the goal of reducing carbon emissions in their city instituted a policy that ran counter to the incentive structure of the average citizen. Waking up an hour earlier one day a week to enter a crowded bus, or adding taxi expenditures to your budget, or having a coworker wake up earlier to pick you up on the other side of town is simply a nuisance. For a middle or upper-middle class family with two vehicles and two incomes, the simple work around involves purchasing an old, nonfuel-efficient vehicle to use once or twice per week with a different license plate number. Politicians failed to understand the complexity of the system and the incentive structure of the average working citizen.

A nation's economy is a complex system, much like the commuter economy of Mexico City. For a central planner, however well intentioned, to claim to know what is best for all stakeholders takes incredible hubris. Oftentimes, they make decisions with incomplete knowledge that lead to unintended consequences. I do not believe that all politicians or central bankers are nefarious or unintelligent people. Most central bankers have Ivy League educations and most politicians have an incredible record of public service. Yet combine a dangerous economic theory with the law of unintended consequences and you get a low growth, low inflation, negative real interest rate zombie economy. You get a bloated financial system, a wealth gap not seen since the 1920s, and mass populism. Economies are normally the interaction of land, labor, capital, and technology on the open market. Western economies are centrally planned on a debt-based perpetual growth model that requires inflation to keep the system afloat.

Most of the lower- and middle-class sense that something is unfair but cannot articulate their discontent. For this reason, populism takes form on the left and right. The root of 21st-century populism is the economic system created post-1971, where the cost of living continuously rises through inflationary policies while wages remain stagnant. Wage earners own less of the pie over time, whereas asset owners own more over time. Most of international relations theory rests on the rational actor model—the simple assumption that individuals and nations make rational social and economic decisions based on the information they have. Placing blame on social media, the millennial generation, the baby-boomer generation, the left, the right, or anything of that matter is simply a scapegoat for a centrally planned economic system that benefits the few at the expense of the many.

In this chapter, we will examine how the Federal Reserve, in an attempt to counter the business cycle, simply doubles down on the debt and easy credit that led to a business cycle downturn in the first place. Overtime, this leads to a lack of economic dynamism and perpetually low growth, similar to Japan and Europe. Next, when the Fed no longer has the tool of manipulating interest rates to create growth, they must rely on increased money printing. This is where the U.S. economy is today. With interest rates at the zero-lower bound, I examine why monetary policy 2.0 is required if the government wants to avoid a deflationary spiral. Bitcoin is the clear winner from this policy because the currency serves as the release valve when interest rates no longer work to stimulate.

Lastly, I ruminate on the potential for monetary policy 3.0—Central Bank Digital Currencies (CBDCs). Using blockchain technology allows for direct to consumer, targeted stimulus. It also allows for easy on-ramps to Bitcoin, Ethereum, and other Decentralized Finance (DeFi) protocols. While some would consider austerity the responsible thing to do, increasing taxes and decreasing spending with the current debt overhang would lead to depression-level human suffering as central bankers have kicked this can down the road for 40 years. For the political class, this is not a feasible solution. Economic central planning has created an unstable financial system and Bitcoin is the insurance policy.

A Dangerous Idea

By manipulating interest rates and increasing the supply of money, the Federal Reserve can prevent recessions and achieve its dual mandate of maintaining high employment and stabilizing prices. Much like Mexico City's "Hoy no circula" program, I will explain how this idea has done more harm than good for any country that adopted it. In the face of economic weakness, global Central Banks act as a counter-cyclical force. They loosen credit and expand the money supply to increase aggregate demand and pull economies out of recessions. Loosening credit is a euphemism for creating more debt, and monetary expansion is a euphemism for currency debasement. This has been the U.S. monetary playbook since the end of the inflationary era of the 1970s.

Following is a chart of the Fed Funds Rate, the interest rate set by the Federal Reserve, over the last 40 years (Figure 3.1). It makes a series of lower highs and lower lows in a perfectly linear downward channel. Why is it that when the economy normalizes, interest rates cannot pass the level of the previous recession? In a recession, corporations and households struggle to make their debt service payments due to reduced economic activity. Normally, this would lead to default or restructuring on behalf of the economic actor. However, with artificially lower rates, these actors can reduce their debt burden by refinancing to survive another day and take advantage of lower rates to take on more debt to create growth. Accompanying a downward channel in rates is an upward channel in corporate, sovereign, and household debt. When interest rates rise again,

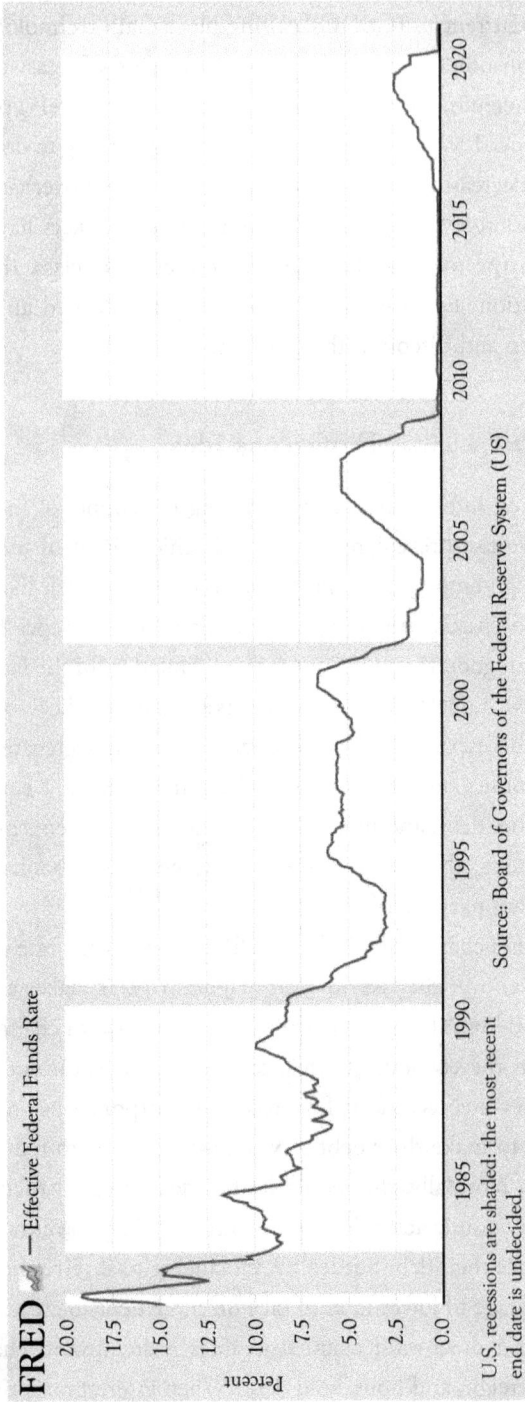

FRED 🔖 — Effective Federal Funds Rate

U.S. recessions are shaded; the most recent end date is undecided.

Source: Board of Governors of the Federal Reserve System (US)

Figure 3.1 Effective federal funds rate since 1980

the economy begins to weaken at a lower rate than the previous recession. This makes intuitive sense. How can companies that struggled to make debt service payments at 800 bps possibly make them at 600 bps and twice the debt load?

As an investor, long bonds has been the best trade for nearly half a century as a play on this countercyclical, kicking the can down the road Fed reaction function. When the economy is weak, stock prices decrease and bond prices increase. The 60/40 stock and bond portfolio has under-pinned institutional finance and retail portfolios for over 40 years because Fed policy created anticorrelation. It also succeeded because rates had room to fall in each recession. In a recession, rates drop an average of 500 bps (or 5 percent). Before the 2020 recession triggered by the corona-virus, the Effective Federal Funds Rate topped at 2.4 percent. When rates are below 5 percent and the Fed needs to stimulate, it relies on the money printer. With the size of the debt burden, interest rates must remain low as even small increases in the interest rate lead to substantial increases in interest payments and defaults. The money printer will play a central role in future stimulus.

Before 2008, interest rates was the primary tool to stabilize the econ-omy and create growth. Once interest rates hit the zero bound for the first time in the Great Financial Crisis of 2008, Central Banks began to rely heavily on a policy of quantitative easing (QE). Today, money creation through QE constitutes the second half of the Central Bank equation. In this policy, Central Banks create money to purchase assets from large banks that free up their balance sheets to support lending and investments. In the United States, these assets include, but are not limited to, government bonds, corporate bonds, and mortgage-backed securities. The Bank of Japan will buy its countries' equities as well and currently owns nearly 80 percent of the Japanese Exchange Traded Fund market and 43 percent of the entire Japanese Government Bond Market. When Central Banks pur-chase these assets, their balance sheet expands. If previous purchases come to maturity faster than new purchases, the balance sheet contracts. From 2008 to the end of 2020, the Federal Reserve Balance Sheet has exploded from $880 million to $7.4 trillion. The money printing will continue at this extraordinary pace in order to stave off a deflationary spiral. Scarcity wins when the global unit of account is abundant. This means taking abundant

Central Bank-created dollars and placing in them in scarce, nonmanipulatable assets. As previously demonstrated, nothing is more scarce than Bitcoin and this concept explains why dollar cost averaging into Bitcoin has outperformed every complex investment strategy that exists today.

In terms of asset prices, QE increases bond prices (thereby decreasing bond yields) and increases stock prices. Bond yields decrease because they see trillions of dollars of artificial demand from the Central Banks. The European Central Bank's QE programs have forced yields negative for the 10-year bond and most government bonds. This means that a purchaser of European government bonds is guaranteed to lose money. Equities rise in a more circuitous manner. While the U.S. Fed does not buy equities, it replaces bonds with cash on the balance sheets of major banks. Well-known primary dealer banks include J.P. Morgan Chase, CitiGroup, Wells Fargo, Goldman Sachs, Morgan Stanley, and so on. While the Fed cannot directly purchase riskier assets such as equities and high yield credit, primary dealer banks can through hedge funds, trading desks, and other market participants. Central Banks target lending but banks tighten lending standards in the face of recessions. Therefore, newly created cash at the Federal Reserve does not become lent out for productive means but sits on bank balance sheets or finds its way to risk assets. The Forex market, buying and selling currency exchange rates for profit, sees $6.6 trillion of daily volume. For comparison, Japanese GDP is $4.9 trillion, German GDP is $3.9 trillion, and South Korea's GDP is $1.6 trillion. In an attempt to increase lending, Central Banks have created an unproductive, hyper-financialized economy and lifted the prices of all financial assets. This is the unintended consequence of misguided policy. Unfortunately, with rates already at zero, money printing programs are the only tool available at the Fed to replace lost capital. QE will only take up a larger share of the Fed equation to spur growth.

If income growth does not exceed debts owed, economic actors cannot make their debt service payments and will default. Therefore, the idea behind monetary policy is to increase growth by slashing the cost of borrowing. In a free market economy, the cost of borrowing is not manipulated by a central authority. There is a free market for the cost of borrowing through a self-regulating mechanism that involves savers and borrowers. More individuals are inclined to save with high interest rates, offering their savings as loanable funds for entrepreneurs to take out loans. Too many savers drive the interest rates lower, incentivizing borrowing. Too many borrowers drive the interest rates higher, incentivizing saving. Central banks attempt to dissuade anyone from saving because that money does not enter the market for consumption or investments. They do this through a high inflation rate and low interest rate, ensuring that your savings will lose value over time if it sat in a bank account. Adopting Bitcoin or any store of value as savings ensures that your money can be spent on your terms.

By manipulating interest rates, U.S. growth becomes debt based, not organic. Debt is deflationary because future income is promised to something that has already been consumed. The more debt one takes on, the larger percentage of current expenditures go to debt and interest payments. Therefore, the greatest consequence of a debt-based growth system is its drag on future growth as we've seen in Europe and Japan—the latter of which has a debt-to-GDP ratio of 250 percent. It's the law of diminishing returns applied to debt-based growth. U.S. government debt-to-GDP increased from 32 percent in 1980 to 106 percent by the end of 2019. All the while the rate of change of growth has declined steadily.

According to a study by Dr. Lacey Hunt of Hoisington Investment Management Company, each dollar of debt produced in 1980 created a rise in GDP of 60 cents. In 1940, with a 42 percent debt-to-GDP ratio compared to 1980's 30 percent, that number was 54 cents. As debt increased substantially following 1980, each dollar of debt went on to create 42 cents of growth in 1989 and 27 cents in 2019. Increased debt creates decreased returns on growth as more of that debt goes to pay interest.[2] Since 1980, each additional dollar of debt went on produce less than half of the original growth.

Another study by the Institute of International Finance in 2018 concluded that it took $185 trillion of debt globally to create $46 trillion of growth. At one-quarter growth to debt, this study aligns with Dr. Hunt's. We have reached debt saturation. We have record levels of debt, interest rates at zero, and more debt creates less growth. Income growth will not exceed debts owed on a significant basis because this debt-fueled growth model has reached its zenith with the cost of borrowing at zero. The next section looks at ways out of this debt trap and why all roads lead to decreasing the debt owed through inflation as opposed to artificially creating growth. Structural flaws in the financial system have created a need for increased money printing. That money printing will be a boon for Bitcoin.

Monetary Policy 2.0

In addition to his role as a fund manager for Bridgewater Associates, Ray Dalio also provides thoughtful books and articles that combine economic history and theory to inform his investment decisions. In his article titled "Paradigm Shifts," Dalio makes the claim that investors will see differences in what typified this decade from the previous decade based on Central Banks reaching the limits of monetary policy. Major themes of the last decade include massive stock market gains, global disinflation, stock buybacks, the rise of passive investing, low GDP growth, low volatility, QE/the expansion of the Fed balance sheet, artificially low interest rates, big tech, and reduced cost of labor.

These themes all relate to one another. QE and low interest rates led to stock market inflation and the rise of passive investing, which is inherently a low volatility strategy. Cheap money also allows for stock buybacks and mergers and acquisitions, further inflating asset prices. Technology monopolies such as Google, Amazon, and Apple reduce economic dynamism through reduced competition and reduce labor costs by displacing labor. Writing in 2019, Dalio then comments on when this paradigm shift will occur:

> I think that it is highly likely that sometime in the next few years, 1) central banks will run out of stimulant to boost the markets and the economy when the economy is weak, and 2) there will be an enormous amount of debt and non-debt liabilities (e.g., pension and health care) that will increasingly be coming due and won't be able to be funded with assets.[3]

With rates at zero, Central Banks can no longer rely on manipulating borrowing costs to increase growth. QE, meanwhile, has proven to favor financial markets over the real economy. How can a country outgrow its debts when there is no growth to be had? The answer is they do not. They eliminate their debt.

In his book, *Principles for Navigating Big Debt Crises*, Dalio offers a four-pronged solution to reducing a debt burden that has become too large. Countries can enact austerity, which entails taxing more and spending less. They can default on their debt and restructure their economies, they can transfer money from the haves to the have-nots through increased taxes on the wealthy and increased social programs, or they can inflate their way out of the debt. They can also use some combination of the four.[4]

To begin with, austerity is politically and economically infeasible. There are no political parties touting fiscal responsibility as evidenced by $6 trillion balance sheet expansion in roughly a decade and the emergence of "deficits don't matter" ideology of Modern Monetary Theory. The government issues bonds to spend money that it does not have at incredibly low rates. The Central Banks, in order to avoid deflation that would force governments to curb spending and create a recession, must print money to purchase these bonds. Under this system, no consequences exist for deficit spending from a political standpoint. Monetary debasement is the economic consequence. Meanwhile, the consequences of voting for austerity as a politician involves being elected out of office. As far as political incentives go, deficit spending will continue.

Economically, the amount of debt in the system with levered financial markets, levered housing markets, levered corporate balance sheets, and Central Banks acting as the buyer only resort for government debt issuances, austerity is not an option. Recessions often act as brushfires, eliminating the nonproductive companies and making way for entrepreneurs to fill the gaps. By combating each recession with lower rates, the Fed did not allow this cleansing to occur. Now, we have a massive, inefficient field that even a small spark could set ablaze. Cutting spending, increasing taxes, or increasing interest rates will have major consequences. For corporations and individuals, it will make debt service payments unmanageable and pop a 40-year debt bubble. Companies will default en masse and we will see a deflation in the price of housing and stocks. It will force the government to cut already underfunded pension system promises and erase the retirement hopes of a generation overallocated to stocks. For governments, it will force them to cut fiscal spending, decreasing the social safety net during an objectively difficult time. Contemporary policy is more about keeping the system afloat after the inefficiencies created by decades of central planning. Rates will remain low and Central Banks will not hesitate if they see the need to inject liquidity. Learning from the Greek example, austerity would collapse prices and any hope for growth while only increasing social tensions.

Secondly, the United States will not default. Countries that own their own printing presses never default because an easier alternative exists to erasing debts—printing the money. I believe the third option, large-scale wealth transfers, will happen to an extent but will not nearly be enough.

I believe the Fed has already signaled that they will inflate the debt away by promising to keep rates at zero through 2022 and target over 2 percent inflation. They will accomplish this by printing more money than is necessary. Under a policy of inflation, dollars in the future are worth less than current dollars. With fixed payments, debtors are paying their debt back with less money than when they received that debt. For example, at 1 percent interest and 3 percent inflation, a debt burden is halved in only 36 years. This is essentially a slow-motion default and less painful way to erase debt.

In the words of Ray Dalio:

> So there will have to be some combination of large deficits that are monetized, currency depreciations, and large tax increases, and these circumstances will likely increase the conflicts between the capitalist haves and the socialist have-nots.[5]

Monetary policy 2.0 will not rely on interest rate manipulation to outpace debt growth. It will rely on inflation to decrease the debt burden because all the growth was had with rates currently at zero. The future will involve currency depreciation, debt monetization, high inflation, de-globalization, increased tension, helicopter money, and increased taxes. The alternative is a painful restructuring and an unwind of the debt spiral. As previously mentioned, the release valve is the currency. Bitcoin will play a larger role in monetary policy 2.0 as the only form of sound money in existence.

Here is an analogy to think about the paradigm shift between current monetary policy to 2.0, then to 3.0. Maslow's hammer is a cognitive bias that states, "When all you have is a hammer, everything looks like a nail." The Federal Reserve had a hammer to counteract the business cycle in interest rates. It smashed them lower and lower as it was their only solution. When rates hit zero, they replaced the interest rate hammer with the money printing hammer. Now in the face of economic weakness, the Federal Reserve prints money and frees up bank balance sheets to create lending. When this hammer proves ineffective, it will be replaced with a scalpel. Processes are in motion for blockchain based CBDCs that can provide targeted stimulus to a desired demographic group. If the money printing hammer benefits Bitcoin by debasing the currency, the CBDC scalpel benefits Bitcoin by digitizing money on a global scale.

Monetary Policy 3.0

The current tool of global Central Banks is the printing press to inflate the debt away. This is the perfect storm for Bitcoin. However, there is one major flaw with QE known as the Cantillon Effect. Due to this flaw, governments are beginning to implement helicopter money in the form of stimulus checks. If the banks will not lend the money the Fed gives them, the government will put the money directly into the pockets of consumers. Monetary policy 3.0 is a blend between monetary and fiscal. Once the technology exists to target a specific demographic group and provide them with stimulus, I believe QE programs will be significantly reduced. The role of the Fed will be to monetize the deficits created by fiscal spending, not to act as it sees fit through changing the interest rate.

The Cantillon Effect was named after Richard Cantillon, an Irish–French economist who first observed this concept in the 18th century. It states that the first recipients of new money benefit the most from monetary expansion because they can spend it before prices rise. Therefore, the infusion mechanism matters greatly. As previously mentioned, the government and primary dealer banks of Wall Street receive the money first through the Fed's bond purchasing program. However, as part of the CARES Act of 2020, the Fed expanded its program and to begin buying an array of corporate bonds in addition to government bonds and mortgage-backed securities.[6] The first recipients include the government, large banks, and large corporations.

That money typically stays in the financial system and influences the prices of financial assets such as stocks, bonds, private equity, and real estate before making its way to the real economy. In fact, governments and large banks receive this money at negative real interest rates and lend it out at higher rates to small banks or small-to-medium-sized businesses. Aside from a mortgage that uses the home as collateral, the average person does not have such easy access to capital. Those without access to capital, those who do not own financial assets, and those with fixed wages such as pensioners, minimum wage earners, and even salaried professionals of the middle class are hurt the most by this top-down approach. The first recipients of printed money have the exorbitant privilege of receiving that money for free and charging interest or routing that money to financial assets if they feel the need to tighten lending standards due to economic uncertainty.

The Cantillon Effect plays itself out through inflation differentials. Freshly printed money nests itself into financial assets and services with easy access to capital. Since 1997, college tuition and hospital services have inflated by roughly 200 percent each. Why? Universities and health care providers can charge exorbitant prices for services as long as the government subsidies and easy lending standards ensure that the bills will be paid. In terms of financial assets, the S&P 500 is up over 300 percent and housing prices, as measured by the Case-Shiller Housing Index, are up 274 percent. Overall inflation, as measured by the Consumer Price Index, increased 62 percent during the same time frame. While abundant goods become cheaper as technological advances reduce production costs, the prices of essential services and financial assets explode. This increases the wealth gap and contributes to the general sense of unfairness felt internationally that led to the rise of populism.

I do not believe this system can continue indefinitely. Central Banks, to their credit, have asked governments for fiscal support as they only have two tools currently to stimulate the economy. Governments responded in 2020 with mass stimulus checks, which I believe serve as a precursor to Universal Basic Income. If governments wish to create inflation in goods other than financial assets and subsidized services, they will need to change the cash infusion mechanism from bond purchases to helicopter money or direct-to-consumer checks. Similar to interest rates or QE, helicopter money is a hammer used to combat deflation. Though the service and travel industries are most affected by a pandemic, stimulus checks will also reach software engineers, lawyers, and those whose professional life saw little or no change from the pandemic. However, this will change in monetary policy 3.0.

The Bank for International Settlements along with seven global Central Banks published a report in October 2020 titled "Central Bank Digital Currencies: foundational principles and core features." The Central Banks of Canada, Japan, Switzerland, the United Kingdom, and the United States all collaborated on this piece and even state, "this report summarizes where they collectively stand."[7] First of all, let's begin with defining a CBDC. The report defines it as "a digital payment instrument, denominated in the national unit of account, that is a direct liability of the central bank." In essence, it is a blockchain-based digital dollar held at the Central Bank as opposed to an individual's personal bank.

Though the report includes many motivations such as financial inclusion and cross-border payments, I believe the section on "facilitating fiscal transfers" constitutes the true calling card of CBDCs. Quickly and without a third party, Central Banks could credit your account with desired stimulus. A digital dollar also allows for "programmable monetary policy." For example, and the report specifically mentions these examples, Central Banks could program an expiry date to the stimulus or conditions such that it must be spent on certain goods or services. It could also target specific demographics such as those who work in the travel or restaurant industries during a pandemic. Using CBDCs, Central Banks can specifically target who or what they want provide stimulus to. It trades their hammer for a scalpel.

Interestingly enough, the report highlights the largest risk of creating CBDCs—disintermediating banks. If everyone holds an account at the Central Bank for the convenience of fiscal transfers, and one can use that account for regular, daily purchases, there is no need for a commercial bank account aside from certain services such as private loans. Additionally, the second of three "foundational principles" listed of CBDCs is coexistence, stating that "central banks have a mandate for stability."

At this point, I remind you of the most dangerous course of action analogy presented in the previous chapter. How could a private money succeed when it undermines the legitimacy of governments that issue currency and banks that charge fees for transactions? Many critics claim that Bitcoin could never succeed because it challenges entrenched powers.

However, it appears the opposite is happening. Central Banks are utilizing blockchain technology to create their own digital currencies, touting coexistence and their mandate for stability while admitting that it undermines traditional banking. Getting the entire population accustomed to online banking on a blockchain-based platform will provide simple on ramps to Bitcoin and other DeFi protocols. I believe that through CBDCs, we are witnessing the transformation from a physical dollars and gold-based system to a digital dollars and Bitcoin-based system.

Conclusion

Bitcoin benefits from this Central Bank trap. For 40 years, Central Banks refused to allow the business cycle to cleanse the economy from a misallocation of resources by dropping interest rates to pull aggregate demand forward. They essentially kicked the can down the road. When the issues of too much debt and too little growth threatened the economy, they doubled down instead of undergoing restructuring. Restructuring at this point will lead to massive deflation and depression-level human suffering.

Global Central Banks are stuck. They need to keep the system afloat and cannot do it with interest rates alone. Therefore, they began using the printing press. However, the printing press is both inefficient and grants exorbitant privilege to governments, large banks, and large corporations through the Cantillon Effect. An overreliance on the printing press with rates at zero provides the perfect storm for Bitcoin's price. Targeted fiscal deposits through CBDCs will complete the transfer from a physical dollar and gold to a digital dollar and Bitcoin.

Understanding the Central Bank trap is why the 60/40 portfolio model of the past will not provide the same results in the future. Bonds perform exceptionally well in an environment where interest rates trend lower. Bonds perform poorly when interest rates have nowhere to go but higher and the threat of inflation constantly looms given the amount of monetary and fiscal expansion. In this environment, real and monetary assets will outperform bonds. Most investors are oblivious to the fact that the western world is reaching the limits of monetary policy and their portfolios are completely unprepared. Future portfolios need to diversify away from credit and into hard assets such as commodities and Bitcoin.

Hard assets constitute the antifragile parts of the portfolio that strengthen with additional currency devaluation and financial experimentation.

While many see gold as the quintessential hard asset, Bitcoin is theoretically superior to gold and its price action compared to gold demonstrates this. If investors buy Bitcoin and gold for the same reasons, and Bitcoin outperforms gold by 10× to 20×, one must wonder why invest in both unless as a hedge against the probability of governments fighting Bitcoin. However, all evidence points to the contrary through blockchain based CBDCs and increased institutional adoption. Thus far, readers should have a mental model to understand Bitcoin, its potential role in portfolio management, and the macroeconomic factors that make it such an attractive asset to own. In the subsequent chapters before discussing Ethereum and Altcoins, I will delve into the specifics of Bitcoin investing to include how to value it and how to invest in it.

CHAPTER 4

Valuing Bitcoin

Many investors hit a wall in their Bitcoin studies that this book attempts to solve. For example, one common complaint is "I cannot value Bitcoin." Investors have a plethora of tools to find the intrinsic value of a specific equity such as discounted cash flow analysis or liquidation value. They can also compare equities on a relative basis through Price to Equity, Price to Book, Return on Invested Capital, and so on. Investors can also calculate the present value of a bond's future coupon payments. Aside from cash flow analysis, bonds are also more straightforward because they offer a clearly advertised yield. Unlike traditional assets, Bitcoin does not have a yield, it does not have a balance sheet, and it does not have a CEO or board of directors to evaluate.

Bitcoin is similar to gold and other commodities in that its price is determined by supply, demand, and ability to retain value over time. Similar to Bitcoin, gold has no shortage of critics. Gold has limited use in production, it has no yield, and is oftentimes considered "going long on fear" as Warren Buffett states. This is due to the fact that in economic turmoil, investors demand a store of value disassociated with the financial system. Aversion to gold is a bias attained from the dominance of the 60/40 portfolio and equity outperformance specifically. It is a bias that mostly clusters around U.S. stock pickers. And why not? Their ideas have proven correct for at least half a century. However, this model is incomplete at best and ignorant at worst. For one, gold has outperformed Berkshire Hathaway's Class A Shares by 117 percent from 2000 to 2020. Likely understanding this, Buffett opened a $565 million position in Barrick Gold in 2020. I present this point for investors to know that mental models can change depending on the information available and to prove that a shiny rock without yield can outperform a portfolio of equities selected by the world's most renowned stock picker depending on the macroeconomic environment.

I remind readers of the Austrian concept of utility versus scarcity value. Most investors focus on utility value. Stocks represent a share of a company that provides economic utility through goods and/or services. Bonds represent the debt of a company or government that provides utility to the investor in coupon payments over a given duration. Real estate provides a bit of both—utility as a good that can provide shelter and rental income, and scarcity depending on the geographic location. Commodities also provide both through industrial uses. However, unlike real estate, they can have wild fluctuations in price based on conditional scarcity due to changes in supply or demand. African swine fever in mainland China in 2018 led to the death of 100 million pigs and a 110 percent increase in the price of pork through the following year. On the demand side, the price of avocados nearly doubled in 2019 alone as it simply became a more popular food for western consumers.

Gold has inherent scarcity, but not conditional scarcity. Both its demand and supply remain relatively constant, though economic conditions can give gold a scarcity premium that investors take advantage of. Current conditions of high money printing constitutes one of these times. Bitcoin has both types of scarcity. It has inherent scarcity in 21 million. However, every four years it goes through a supply shock where the number of incoming coins gets halved. It can also undergo demand shocks as Bitcoin funds become approved for trading on public markets and as corporations with large balance sheets begin adopting it as a treasury asset. Readers should understand that the valuation of Bitcoin is based on understanding the supply and adoption rates. However, we could also use technical analysis and network analysis to determine fair value for Bitcoin and whether it is under- or overvalued. This chapter contains several ways to identify the value of Bitcoin—stock-to-flow (SF), market cap/realized cap, the Mayer multiple, the number of days since all-time high, the Relative Strength Index (RSI), the Power Law, and network statistics such as miner capitulation, the hash rate, and the number of active addresses. An investor with these tools will be well equipped to determine Bitcoin's location in its price cycle.

Stock-to-Flow Model

The SF model was first introduced in 2019 by a pseudonymous Dutch investor through a blog post titled "Modeling Bitcoin's Value with Scarcity."[1] The chart overlays the monthly SF ratio with market value. Naturally, the higher the ratio, the more scarce the asset. The more scarce the asset, the higher its market value. The relationship between gold, silver, palladium, and platinum clearly demonstrates this. The following chart (Figure 4.1) shows the parsimonious relationship between the annual SF model price and Bitcoin price, posted by Plan B in early 2020. Though this section briefly summarizes the model and its statistical findings, I highly recommend reading the primary source if readers wish to learn more.

The study finds a statistically significant relationship between annual SF ratio and market value with an R-squared of 0.95. This model translates to a price per coin of $100,000 following the halving in May 2020. The model was updated in 2020, removing time and treating each halving as a different asset. That means Bitcoin with an SF of 3.3 was separated from 10.2 and separated again from 25.1. The author considered the halving as phase transitions. Bitcoin with an SF of 3.3 and market capitalization of $58 million was mostly a tool for anonymous online payments, while an SF of 25.1 and market capitalization of $114 billion is considered the financial asset phase. Similar to the original version, the model kept data on gold and silver for comparison. The result? A more statistically significant relationship at 0.99 and a revised price target of $288,000 by the end of the 2020–2024 cycle.[2]

What we have is a range of outcomes based on Bitcoin's scarcity—from the author's original price target of $55,000 to the updated $288,000 based on supply dynamics alone. Bringing demand into the equation tells a different story. The price of Bitcoin tends to overshoot or undershoot the model significantly based on adoption rates. For example, the price in the March 2020 lows hit $3,000 while the model had a price of $8,000 due to an acute sell-off at the beginning of the COVID-19 pandemic. Investors may see some versions of the model that contain volatility bands to account for exogenous shocks. A cycle repeat graph demonstrates what the price of Bitcoin would be if it followed the previous cycle exactly. Every cycle tends to experience a blow off top and reach bubble territory toward the end. The cycle repeat chart shows a top of $333,069 in October 2021. Though some data tends to suggest that each cycle has a lower top than the previous one, which makes intuitive sense based on the idea that volatility will stabilize over time with more adoption, not enough cycles have played out to confirm or deny the assertion. The current cycle brought institutional capital, whereas retail investors drove the previous one.

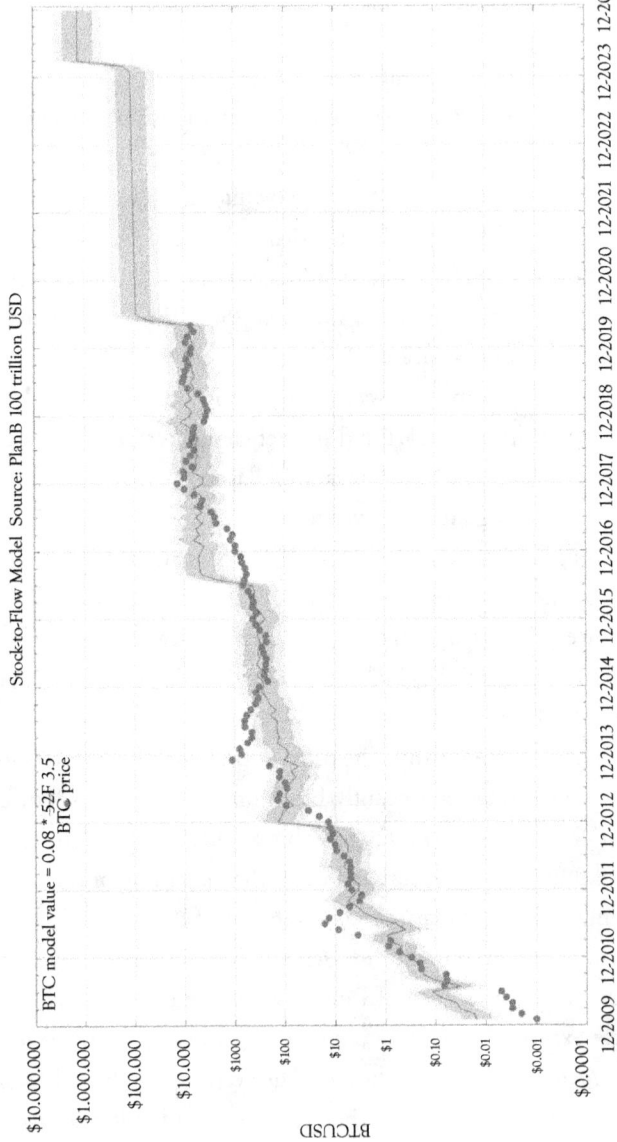

Figure 4.1 Stock-to-flow model

Investors can model Bitcoin's value using the SF ratio. Though which one? Depending on the variables used, the model shows values of $55,000, $100,000, or $288,000 for the 2020–2024 price cycle alone. Though the largest value demonstrates the most statistical significance, I believe investors should couple the SF ratio with other valuation metrics. The central concept of the model will always make intuitive sense, even if it breaks one day. Assuming constant demand, price will increase as supply gets halved every four years, and there will always be demand for hard money as global Central Banks race to devalue their currencies. For some investors, this is Occam's razor applied to Bitcoin's price action. Though many have attempted to disprove the model, the price of Bitcoin has continued to track it with uncanny accuracy. As a long-term investment, the model states that investing in the 2020–2024 price cycle is still considered early entry. Investors can track where the current price stands in relation to the model's value on websites such as digitalik.net, lookintobitcoin.com, and more.

Market Cap/Realized Cap (MVRV)

This ratio compares Bitcoin's market capitalization to its realized capitalization. The market cap is the number of coins circulating multiplied by the price per coin. It constitutes the value of the entire network. Unlike equities, there exists a fraction of Bitcoin in circulation that are lost and coins on the network that have never moved since initial purchase. This occurs mostly for three reasons: (1) early investors forgot their private key; (2) physical cold storage investors, a topic discussed in the next chapter, that lost the physical hard drive, USB drive, or whichever method of storage; and (3) early investors who never sell. Experts believe that up to 15 percent of Bitcoins are in fact lost and will never enter circulation.

Realized cap takes unspent transaction output into account (UTXO). It gives an average price paid for all coins on the network at the time they last moved on the blockchain. It is the value whereby most Bitcoin investors purchased their coins. This metric matters because investors can use it to gauge when most participants entered the market and if the price is over-or undervalued. Knowing the average entry point for most market participants provides an advantage to the investor. Taking behavioral economics into account, most participants will experience a fear of missing out and enter the bull market much too late. A variant of the Market Cap/Realized Cap (MVRV) is MVRV with a z-score (MVRV-z). A z-score is the number of standard deviations above or below the mean.

Here is the takeaway from this metric: if MVRV-z is below one, then the exchange traded price is below the average price of all Bitcoins paid. This makes Bitcoin a tremendous buying opportunity and a value below one only occurs in the troughs of bear markets. If the MVRV-z score has a weekly close above five, there is a 94.36 percent chance of reversal. Five and above is overvalued territory. However, as previously mentioned, Bitcoin peaks usually escape all rationality and well overshoot SF model prices. Bitcoin enters virtuous cycles that create both blow-off tops and vicious cycles that create an average 84 percent crash from the all-time high. The MVRV-z peaked at 11.1 in 2011, 11.4 in 2014, and 11.5 in 2018. The 2014 bull market actually reached a 12.8 level before crashing by nearly 50 percent, consolidating for five months, and then reaching a new all-time high just above $1,000. Therefore, while 5 is overvalued, 10 and 11 is bubble territory. Expect an imminent, dramatic correction when the z-score reaches these levels. This metric can be found at charts.woobull.com.

The Mayer Multiple

The next few valuation metrics focus on technical analysis—not supply-based price modeling or on-chain metrics such as average price paid per coin. Similar to MVRV, the Mayer Multiple also determines whether Bitcoin is overbought, oversold, or fairly priced. It divides the price of Bitcoin by the 200-day moving average. After statistical analysis on this metric, Trace Mayer, the investor who first proposed the model, determined that buying at multiples below 2.4 yielded the best results. While a value over 2.4 on the Mayer Multiple signals overvalued territory, a Mayer Multiple below one signals undervalued territory and a bear market as the market price dipped below the 200-day moving average.

Days Since All-Time High or Days Until the Next Halving

This metric takes advantage of Bitcoin's predictably cyclical nature. In the last two market cycles, it took Bitcoin roughly 1,000 days to reach a new all-time high from the previous cycle top. In the 2014 cycle, that number was much lower at 614. Once the price surpasses the previous all-time high, it took 9 to 10 months for the price to peak for that cycle. The price also tends to peak roughly 900 days before the subsequent halving event. This metric is significant because it prevents investors from selling early when faced with volatility. Bitcoin will significantly correct several times before the cycle top. Taking time into account in previous cycles helps investors determine whether a price dip is a correction or in fact the beginning of a bear market. Bitcoin reached its all-time high in late November 2020. This tells investors that the price of the current cycle should peak in the September–October 2021 timeframe. Supplanting previous cycles onto the current one is a crude metric, but helpful when combined with other metrics. A variant of this metric is blocks since all-time high. As previously mentioned, Bitcoin tends to peak 70,000 blocks after the halving. Bitcoin contains both programmed scarcity and pro-grammed cyclicality with a four-year supply shock. Price action has thus far been very predictable, though it may not always be the case.

The Relative Strength Index (RSI)

RSI is a momentum indicator commonly used with technical analysts trading equities. It is an oscillator between zero and one-hundred that investors can overlay to a chart pattern to determine overbought and oversold conditions. Thirty and below indicates oversold while 70 and above indicates overbought. RSI takes 14 days of trading data and the average percent gain or loss. It increases with the number of consecutively positive trading days and vice versa. Why is this simple metric important for Bitcoin investors? Because the previous three bull markets closed with an RSI of 99, 97, and 97 respectively. Meanwhile the bear markets ended with values of 48, 43, and 42 respectively. Investors should remain glued to this number and use it to distinguish between corrections and peaks. The probability of a price dip with RSI at 80 being the cycle top is highly unlikely.

The Power Law

Since its inception, Bitcoin has fit a log-based channel of support and resistance. The conclusion of this chapter will explain my theory on why

Bitcoin is such a technical trader's paradise. However, suffice to say, it contains very pure price signals. Even in the sell-off of March 2020, Bitcoin touched its long-term support channel to bounce back to its linear regression fit. In agreement with the SF model, the current resistance channel on the chart indicates a value of around $100,000 throughout 2021. Investors should keep the long-term chart in mind, or use its oscillator that examines deviation from the standard regression of the Power Law where values have historically fallen between −1 and 1. Both metrics can also be found on digitalik.net.

Miner Capitulation, Difficulty Adjustments, and the Hash Rate

Investors will often complain of Bitcoin's volatility and I concede on this point. Bitcoin is undoubtedly volatile. However, volatility is a two-way street, and Bitcoin's volatility is heavily skewed to the upside. To investors who note this feature yet still cannot stomach a 20 percent drop in as little as a week, I recommend a smaller allocation, appropriate diversification, and a long-term time horizon. Bitcoin bear markets usually begin with an 84 percent price drop and bull markets end on face-ripping rallies with over 10x multiple expansion. For those who understand the asset, these drops serve as incredible buying opportunities. Bitcoin is incredibly volatile due to its small market cap, where large movements of money tend to have immediate impacts on price, and due to mining dynamics. This section is more technical, but important for any potential Bitcoin investor.

Miner capitulation is not a valuation metric per se, but an integral component to understand price volatility and can give insight into the health of the network and status of the cycle. Similar to any business, Bitcoin miners have operating costs. Miners vary in size from industrial to small-sized operations. Miners with incredibly low electricity costs and industrial-sized processing power have an advantage over nonindustrial mining operations. When the price of Bitcoin falls beyond a certain point, small miners cannot cover their operating costs with their Bitcoins mined. Once this occurs, their operation becomes obsolete and they become forced sellers. Lower price action begets lower price action as more miners cannot cover operating costs. Difficulty adjustments occur to stop this vicious spiral, and in the end, only the miners with superior equipment and low electricity costs survive. New miners will then enter the network over time.

Difficulty adjustments is when the network adjusts to make the proof of work algorithm more or less complicated. It occurs every 2,016 blocks, or roughly two weeks. If the hash rate is lower, meaning there are less miners online, the adjustment is downward. A simpler algorithm takes less processing power, increasing the profit margins of miners on the network. Due to difficulty adjustments, mining will never become unprofitable for all miners. It also prevents too many miners from going offline thereby keeping the network operational. Think about it as such, if one restaurant goes out of business, it signals that the entire industry is facing pressure. To account for this, food vendors decrease prices to increase profit margins and keep the restaurants running. Difficulty adjustments also have bottoms—moments in time when the proof-of-work calculation is easiest to solve. Difficulty bottoms provide buying opportunities, although the network will occasionally undergo negative difficulty adjustments mid-cycle due to a sell-off. Typically, Bitcoin price will peak at roughly 70,000 blocks after the halving. Investors and traders can profit from Bitcoin without ever knowing these technicalities. However, these details are worth mentioning.

The hash rate is a measure of processing power on the network and a proxy for the amount of operational miners. It is measured in Terahashes (one trillion calculations) per second. A hash ribbon overlays several moving averages of the hash rate. Commonly used moving averages include the 200-day, 90-day, 60-day, 25-day, down to the 9-day moving average. A compressed or inverted hash ribbon indicates that miners are going offline. An inverted hash ribbon, whereby a recent moving average such as the 9-day crosses below a later one such as the 60-day, indicates that the hash rate has dropped significantly and to expect significant selling pressure due to miner capitulation. Eventually, difficulty adjustments will bring this metric back to equilibrium. Meanwhile, a clear, upward trending channel in the hash ribbon indicates a healthy bull market.

The interplay between processing power on the network, price action, difficulty adjustments, and miner capitulation can take chapters to explain thoroughly. Though this book does not intend to be overly technical, even a baseline understanding of these concepts gives the investor a significant advantage over those who only examine SF or technical indicators.

Bitcoin has predictable, programmed cyclicality through its halving cycles. Though nuance exists from cycle to cycle, the overarching theme of absolute scarcity punctuated by conditional scarcity remains intact. By way of analogy, if an investor knew that roughly every four years a wildfire in Brazil would destroy half of the country's coffee crop, he or she would easily front run that event. The price of coffee would be extremely cyclical. However, assuming demand stays constant, allocating even a small portion of one's portfolio to coffee to take advantage of this dynamic simply makes sense.

Number of Active Addresses

In truth, this final metric has less predictive power but can be used to understand Metcalfe's Law and get a sense for animal spirits. The number of active Bitcoin addresses tends to increase linearly, while the price increases exponentially. As each node in the network provides value to all other nodes, this is Metcalfe's Law at work. However, the main use of this metric involves getting a sense for mass adoption. At the peak of the 2017 cycle, Bitcoin had 1,283,917 active addresses. The peak in late 2013 was 197,974 active addresses. One key characteristic of a bubble is mass participation. After rallying from $25,000 to $40,000 from December 2020 to January 2021, several pundits were quick to determine that Bitcoin is in another bubble similar to 2018 and call for an imminent crash. The active address count at that time was 1,068,910; not yet surpassing the 2017 peak. This analysis tells me that we are nowhere near the euphoric, mass adoption mania that typically characterizes bull market tops.

Though I am not saying that each cycle must have a 10× increase in the number of active addresses, this metric has not surpassed 2017 levels. The introduction of third-party trusts and ETFs will certainly muddy this metric in the future. As it currently stands, this metric has not reached euphoric levels indicative of a top, and $40,000 is still mid-cycle. Investors studying these metrics in future cycles can easily apply the same logic.

Conclusion

Because Bitcoin is such a young market with a diminutive market cap and low financial meddling in terms of future contracts, structured products, artificial demand, and the like, it does not have distorted price signals. From a technical perspective, Bitcoin is a very pure market. Though I will always recommend holding as a long-term investment, Bitcoin is a trader's paradise due to its pure price signals. As previously mentioned, the introduction of institutional finance to the Bitcoin market will muddy many of these metrics in the future.

Many investors claim that they do not understand how to determine the value of Bitcoin when a plethora of tools exist from a fundamental and technical standpoint. In my personal experience, most investors who claim this simply have not done their due diligence. Combining the aforementioned tools helps investors understand Bitcoin price cycles and paints a clear picture as to its current position in the cycle. SF provides a supply-based model of future price action though it assumes constant demand. Investors will have two primary complaints regarding the SF model. First, they will claim that this ratio is meant to determine the price of industrial commodities and not financial assets. This claim is nonsense because demand is demand—whether for industrial production or as a financial asset. Secondly, they will claim that the model's upward adjustments from the initial $55,000 target give it less legitimacy. Though the models with higher price targets do have a higher coefficient of determination, the wildly diverse price target is an understandable point of frustration. However, enough other tools exist to make this point negligible as long as the investor understands scarcity dynamics as a concept.

Investors can couple their understanding with on-chain metrics such as MVRV and its z-score. They can use purely technical indicators such as RSI, support and resistance levels from the Power Law, or the Mayer Multiple. They can use previous length of cycles to assist with days from all-time high or behavioral gauges such as the number of active addresses. Lastly, they can get deep in the weeds with network information such as hash rates and difficulty adjustments. Investors cannot value a monetary network as they would a stock or bond. Those whose mental models prevent them from expanding their base of knowledge will simply be left out in what has the potential to be the greatest transfer of wealth in history as early retail investors front-run the coming institutional wave of money.

Lastly, I would like to give a succinct example of how an investor can combine these metrics in the middle of a bull market. Long-term investors should be less concerned with metrics of overvaluation or undervaluation, yet they play an important role in portfolio rebalancing. Following a very strong month at the time of this writing, Bitcoin's RSI value sits at 87, its Mayer Multiple at 2.3, and its MVRV-z score at 6.3, though it has only been one month since it surpassed the previous all-time high and the SF model of a $100,000 price target by the end of 2021 is still on track. Combining this with the previous analysis of blocks following the difficulty bottom and number of active addresses tells me that we are mid-cycle; however, price action has accelerated too far, too fast. A pull-back and several weeks of sideways consolidation would be healthy given slightly overvalued conditions. Writing in early 2021, I believe we still have months to go before these indicators truly scream sell and the price should therefore continue to appreciate over the course of 2021. Due to Bitcoin's predictable cyclicality, I do not recommend annual rebalancing, but rebalancing based on the previously mentioned factors. However, a portion of the portfolio should always be held in Bitcoin.

CHAPTER 5

How to Invest in Bitcoin

This chapter details ways to invest and store Bitcoin while the next chapter will address Bitcoin counterarguments before the book delves into Ethereum and Altcoins. I separate Bitcoin from other cryptocurrencies for reasons that will become clear in later chapters. When purchasing Bitcoin, investors have several options: (1) traditional brokerage account options such as a trust, trading futures contracts, or investing in companies with high exposure; (2) an online Bitcoin wallet typically held with an exchange; (3) an offline Bitcoin wallet that physically stores the asset through methods such as a hard drive, thumb drive, or paper wallet. The terms *hot* and *cold wallets* are synonymous with online and offline storage. Between hot and cold wallet options involve multisignature wallets—those that are held online but have added security because they require multiple keys to authorize any transaction. Each option provides trade-offs between ownership of coins, ease of use, and security. The choice in method of investment usually stems from an investor's personal beliefs regarding the trade-offs above and level of subscription to the principles of Bitcoin purists.

Traditional Brokerage Account Options

Currently, the simplest way to add Bitcoin exposure to an investor's portfolio is through the Grayscale Bitcoin Investment Trust, ticker $GBTC. Though an ETF option does not yet exist, it surely will in the coming years as regulations become solidified. The trust privately owns and stores over 600,000 Bitcoin at the time of this writing and continues to buy at a breakneck pace as demand for the trust increases. There are some advantages to purchasing shares of a publicly traded Bitcoin Trust as opposed to actual Bitcoin. For one, an investor can hold it in retirement accounts such as a Traditional Individual Retirement Account (IRA) or Roth IRA, which they cannot do with the actual asset. This comes with the inherent tax advantage of Bitcoin exposure disguised as a tradable equity in a tax deferred account. Meanwhile, selling Bitcoin in a hot wallet will incur capital gains similar to any other asset.

For investors that desire Bitcoin as a portfolio hedge against inflation or an uncorrelated asset that complements a portfolio of stocks, bonds, commodities, and the like, it helps to have one account managing these positions as opposed to transferring back and forth between a digital wallet and brokerage account. For new investors in the space, a publicly traded fund also eliminates the security versus ownership dilemma that many Bitcoin investors face. There is no need to make a decision about a hot wallet, cold wallet, or multisignature storage. There is also no need to memorize or store private keys. These decisions are pawned off to the experts at Grayscale who secure their Bitcoin offline for a fee—just as a gold trust would with physical storage of gold.

Investors should understand that $GBTC is a grantor trust, not an ETF. The fund is not registered with the Securities and Exchange Commission (SEC) under the Investment Company Act of 1940 and trades over the counter. For many in the Bitcoin community, an SEC-approved ETF is the holy grail given that it provides seamless on-ramps for institutional investors. For example, Merrill Lynch has banned clients and advisors from purchasing the fund since 2018, citing "concerns pertaining to suitability and eligibility standards of this product."[1] Though barring exposure to Bitcoin for its clients will likely backfire by condemning clients to underperformance, the concerns given the trust's status as unregistered with the SEC and traded over the counter does serve as a major obstacle for some would-be institutional investors.

The SEC rejected the first Bitcoin ETF proposal in 2013 and continued to reject proposals citing various reasons. In the 2017 rejection of the Winkelvoss twins' proposal, owners of the Gemini exchange, the SEC cited lack of regulation and the potential for "manipulative acts and practices in this market."[2] As more experienced institutional investment management and ETF firms file applications with the SEC, such as the VanEck proposal that will see a decision in 2021, I believe a fully registered Bitcoin fund or ETF is inevitable. To address previously stated SEC concerns, increasing price action will visit increased regulation. Additionally, increased market capitalization will prevent market whales from creating volatile price action by entering and exiting the market. Until an ETF proposal becomes fully registered, Grayscale's Investment Trust best solves the desire for Bitcoin exposure in traditional brokerage accounts. However, this option also comes with disadvantages.

Grayscale charges an annual fee of 2 percent. While exchanges may charge a fee for transactions, they do not have annual fees for simply holding Bitcoin. The second disadvantage is that the fund oftentimes trades at a premium to the Bitcoin spot price that varies depending on demand. Though the premium tends to remain between 1 and 15 percent, it can rise to extraordinary levels. Near the 2017 peak, $GBTC traded at nearly a 100 percent premium to the spot price. That constitutes buying one Bitcoin for the price of two. On the other hand, $GBTC will trade at a discount to the spot price under heavy selling pressure, and this acts as a barometer for oversold conditions. An ETF that tracks the price would reduce the premium and discount arbitrage. Potential investors to the fund should take fees and the premium into account before making a purchase.

Traders can use the futures market to gain Bitcoin exposure as well. Billionaire hedge fund manager Paul Tudor Jones went public with his support for Bitcoin in mid-2020. In his published Market Outlook, Jones first begins by stating his belief that there will be a "great monetary inflation" caused by unprecedented Fed balance sheet expansion and the unquestioned "direct monetization of massive fiscal spending" following the COVID-19 pandemic.[3] Based on this thesis, he graded several stores of value on four criteria: retaining purchasing power over time, perceived trustworthiness, liquidity, and portability. Assets studied included gold, the 2s30s yield curve, Bitcoin, TIPS breakevens, the tech heavy NASDAQ exchange, U.S. cyclicals, and more. Based on this criteria, Bitcoin scored a 43 compared to gold's 62 based mostly on its liquidity and portability premium. While admittedly less proven than gold to Jones, Bitcoin's market capitalization was only 7 percent of gold's at the time of Jones's report, demonstrating immense upside potential. Due to the low market cap, Jones also states that investing in Bitcoin is akin to investing early in one of the infamous FAANG stocks—Facebook, Amazon, Apple, Netflix, and Google.

I convey Jones's story because the legendary fund manager gains exposure through trading Bitcoin futures. The Chicago Board Options Exchange (CBOE) began offering Bitcoin contracts on December 10, 2017. Again, this option trades asset ownership for price exposure on traditional brokerage accounts through brokers such as TDAmeritrade and Interactive-Brokers. For experienced futures traders, this may well be the best option. However, there is a third option for gaining Bitcoin exposure that does not involve the futures markets and non-SEC approved funds—purchasing shares of companies with known Bitcoin exposure.

Individual equity exposure to Bitcoin varies depending on the company. At the end of 2020, 5.79 percent of all Bitcoin, or 1,216,188 coins, are held on the treasury accounts of companies. Many of these companies are publicly traded. Therefore, the most circuitous route to gain Bitcoin exposure, and less risky route for skeptics, involves purchasing publicly traded shares of a company that has allocated a percentage of its treasury balance away from dollars and into Bitcoin. Companies do this because inflationary policies act as a tax against cash holdings. They also desire exposure to the massive upside potential that Bitcoin offers while only sacrificing a small percentage of the balance sheet. This trend of companies moving small portions of their balance sheets to Bitcoin will accelerate in the future. The companies that I will name shortly have the first-mover advantage.

This section will focus on companies listed on U.S. exchanges, although Canada and Europe have several companies with high Bitcoin treasuries as well. The figures listed were gathered at the end of 2020 and the balance sheets of these companies have surely changed since. Investors can focus on percentage of the balance sheet allocated to Bitcoin or number of Bitcoins outstanding. Square Inc. ($SQ), a commerce-based financial services platform and parent company of CashApp, has the second largest Bitcoin treasury for companies listed in the United States with 4,709 Bitcoin but only 0.2 percent of its balance sheet. The listed company with the third largest Bitcoin treasury is Riot Blockchain, Inc. ($RIOT), a Bitcoin mining operation out of Montana. It has 1,175 outstanding, though a larger 2.7 percent of its treasury in Bitcoin.

The company that has wholeheartedly adopted the Bitcoin Standard as its reserve asset is Michael Saylor's MicroStrategy Incorporated ($MSTR). MicroStrategy owns over 70,000 Bitcoin and roughly one-third of 1 percent of all Bitcoin in existence at the end of 2020. Given Saylor's unwavering conviction, I expect this number will continue increasing. Many investors will buy MicroStrategy as a proxy for Bitcoin, without knowing anything of its business intelligence services. For investors who choose this route, I highly recommend understanding the company itself and the service it provides. MicroStrategy's CEO, Michael Saylor, has laid out his reasoning in several written works and podcasts. He did not want to hold a large cash balance due to the macroeconomic factors reiterated throughout this book and he did not feel compelled to make a large acquisition or hastily use his cash when he saw little opportunities in the market. His solution was to put his treasury on the Bitcoin Standard to keep his reserves from depreciating while he awaited opportunities.[4] Investors in MicroStrategy are investing in a business analytics software company that made the decision to adopt Bitcoin as its reserve asset—they are not directly investing in Bitcoin. The market has rewarded the company greatly. Less than six months after the announcement, the company's stock surged nearly 200 percent.

Current Bitcoin options for a traditional brokerage account include the Grayscale Bitcoin Investment Trust, trading on a futures account, or investing in Bitcoin-friendly companies. These options provide the greatest ease of use for traditional investors. However, disadvantages include service fees, premiums paid, and the fact that you do not own these Bitcoin as you would with a personal wallet. I would equate this to a Gold Trust or having real estate exposure through a Real Estate Investment Trust (REIT) as opposed to owning gold and renting homes yourself. If owned through a fund, the asset truly belongs to the fund and the investor has a claim to that asset. The next option, an online custodial wallet, is both easy to use and provides more of a sense ownership to the investor.

Hot Wallets—Custodial and Noncustodial

Investors draw a multitude of parallels between Bitcoin and physical gold—storage is no different. Custodial wallets connected to the Internet is equivalent to trusting a third party to store your gold. For purists who want personal custody of an asset outside of the financial system, trusting a third party defeats the purpose of owning Bitcoin and gold alike. Why? Because a security breach could occur in the gold vault, the storage company could go rogue and take off with your gold, or the government could outlaw the storage of physical gold and the vault will be forced to comply. Though I would handicap these as low probability events with Bitcoin, they exist within the realm of possibility. An individual who stores his or her physical gold at home in a personal vault does not have such concerns. The same logic applies to Bitcoin storage.

Exchange wallets serve as examples of popular custodial wallets. Popular exchanges include Coinbase, Kraken, and Gemini. They are exchanges that allow users to purchase Bitcoin or other cryptocurrencies and store their assets on a wallet held with the exchange. Both the user and the company have access to the private keys. The phrase "not your keys, not your coins" is popular among Bitcoin purists to signify that these companies are in fact the owners of your Bitcoin. Why would a Bitcoin investor allow a trusted third party to own their coins? For the lay investor with only a few Bitcoin or a percentage of a Bitcoin, for those who regularly trade crypto, or those who use it for purchases, custodial storage makes sense. It also makes sense if you do not trust in your own ability to store your Bitcoin offline or wish to transfer some coins offline when the wallet value reaches a certain amount. Cold storage is undoubtedly more secure but investors risk losing their private keys—just as a gold bar kept at home could be physically lost or stolen.

Having a custodial wallet is similar to a regular brokerage account. Users have a username, password, and typically a second-tier verification system such as a pin or randomized authenticator code. They can link their debit or credit account to make purchases instantaneously from a mobile phone or computer. Verifying one's identity also provides extra benefits such as increased spending limits and the ability to send or receive crypto with other wallets. As opposed to a share price, these wallets show the number of coins held in your wallet and the entire portfolio value. Similar to a brokerage account, a third party getting access to your username, password, and code can withdraw your funds. The exchange may also become bogged down with high activity and prevent immediate settlement of trades. Lastly, and most importantly, users of custodial wallet risk exchange hacks.

While a Bitcoin held offline cannot be hacked, exchanges that hold Bitcoin can. In 2019, the popular Binance cryptocurrency exchange witnessed hackers steal $40 million of Bitcoin in an orchestrated attack that used phishing, viruses, and other sophisticated methods. I remind readers of two facts to mitigate the likelihood of losing Bitcoin. Firstly, know the security and storage system of the exchanges. Large exchanges will typically hold most of their coins in cold storage, have multifaceted authenticity measures, and sophisticated firewalls. The latter two can be said of any brokerage account. I recommend that individuals with large Bitcoin balances use both hot and cold storage—in a similar manner to a checking account readily available for spending and a savings account held offline for emergency situations. Secondly, much of the Bitcoin infrastructure is unproven. Though not the wild west of yesteryear where hackers stole 7 percent of the entire Bitcoin market capitalization from the Mt. Gox exchange in 2014, the threat of hackers stealing through exchanges is still real. Exchanges become more secure with each passing year and most exchanges have had zero security issues. Mt. Gox is short for Magic: The Gathering Online Exchange. The exchange was initially created for customers to buy and sell cards of a fantasy card game. Today's exchanges are not repurposed trading card websites but sophisticated systems that use a balance of hot storage, cold storage, firewalls, and more.

Custodial wallets provide incredible ease of use and a greater sense of coin ownership than traditional brokerage methods. Investors do not see a ticker and price but own a number of Bitcoin custodied by an exchange. They can easily buy, sell, and spend Bitcoin, but this option requires trust in a third party similar to trusting your online broker or a physical gold vault company. This is the most common option for Bitcoin investors; however, noncustodial software and multisignature wallets are both held online and do not require trust in an exchange.

Software wallets downloaded to your desktop exist to allow the owner to have sole custody his or her private key. Essentially, your private key serves as your login information to access your Bitcoin. The software encrypts and stores your private key, but the company does not have access. This trades convenience for greater individual responsibility and safety. In this option, your Bitcoin are as secure as your personal security practices. Multisignature technology is another trustless way to store Bitcoin online. As opposed to a single private key, users can have three keys stored on three different devices. They will need two of the three keys to access their account. If one gets stolen or compromised, their coins are still safe assuming they have the other two keys.

I believe that for the average investor entering the Bitcoin landscape, using a custodial wallet with an exchange will suffice because it provides greater ease of use and optionality if the owner one day wishes to transfer to a more secure wallet. Transferring to cold storage is not possible through shares of a Bitcoin trust. Noncustodial wallets require a greater degree of individual responsibility and some technical knowledge. Only those with a significant amount of net worth wrapped in Bitcoin or traditionalists who want a truly bankless experience have reason for self-custodied wallets. Twenty-first-century custodial practices are secure, though I believe that the reader should know his or her options when it comes to buying and storing Bitcoin. If the investor trusts an online brokerage account, they will likely trust a custodial wallet or third-party trust.

Cold Storage

The process of storing your Bitcoin offline begins with choosing a method. The most popular method is purchasing a hardware wallet such as Ledger Nano or Trezor and transferring your Bitcoin to the physical wallet. Other methods include paper wallets, desktop wallets, or a USB drive. These hardware wallets must be stored in a safe, secure location. Additionally, some physical wallet options are not waterproof, fireproof, and cannot be restored if destroyed. If maintaining physical custody of your Bitcoin sounds stressful, perhaps a custodial wallet serves as your best option. Though cold storage is undoubtedly the most secure storage method because it does not involve a third party, it risks physical destruction, loss, and theft. The owner substitutes digital and counterparty risk for physical risk. Truly, the trade-off is that simple. As previously mentioned, those with a significant number of coins should diversify their storage methods between self-custody and custodial wallets.

Conclusion

The emphasis on private key ownership among Bitcoin circles originates from its anarcho-capitalist origins. Bitcoin was created in January 2009 as a trustless currency and digital analog to gold. Though the gold narrative has surpassed the trust narrative with the introduction of valuation metrics such as the SF ratio, the trustless feature is what drew early Bitcoin adopters. In the words of Bitcoin's founder, Satoshi Nakamoto:

> The root problem with conventional currency is all the trust that's required to make it work. The central bank must be trusted not to debase the currency, but the history of fiat currencies is full of breaches of that trust. Banks must be trusted to hold our money and transfer it electronically, but they lend it out in waves of credit bubbles with barely a fraction in reserve. We have to trust them with our privacy, trust them not to let identity thieves drain our accounts.[5]

Satoshi also differentiates Bitcoin from previous Internet currencies when he focuses on the decentralized and trustless nature of blockchain technology and proof-of-work.

> A lot of people automatically dismiss e-currency as a lost cause because of all the companies that failed since the 1990's. I hope it's obvious it was only the centrally controlled nature of those systems that doomed them. I think this is the first time we're trying a decentralized, non-trust-based system.[6]

The genesis block, the first ever Bitcoin block mined by Satoshi, contained a political message on it. It said, "The Times 03/Jan/2009 Chancellor on brink of second bailout for banks." Bitcoin's origin was more of an anarcho-capitalist political movement than an asset class. It was created in the wake of the bank bailouts of the 2008 Global Financial Crisis and sold as the ideological antithesis to Central Banking. It was against monetary debasement, fractional reserve banking, and rent-seeking practices of governments and banks. It was pro sound money, independence, and privacy. Due to this, it shares an ideological link with physical gold investors and has a market in the investment world. As monetary debasement accelerates, Bitcoin becomes a more attractive asset because Bitcoin was created to counter monetary debasement.

Today, early Bitcoin investors constitute the loud minority. Satoshi created an investable asset based on an ideological movement. However, there is a constant tension between the original ideology and price appreciation. Price appreciation invites more government regulation and institutional adoption from Wall Street. This invites less privacy and independence. My guess is that as the price appreciates and more stakeholders get involved, the "not your keys, not your coins" ideology will become less prevalent. Though an ideological loss for early adopters, they will certainly gain monetarily.

Introductory crypto investors who want a portfolio hedge or exposure to an asymmetric asset class should stick to traditional brokerage options or custodial wallets with a trusted exchange. Those who have completely adopted the Bitcoin Standard as their *modus operandi* or early investors who have a large amount of their net worth in Bitcoin should rely on a mix of hot and cold storage. Before moving funds to cold storage or any form of self-custody, the investor should research best security practices in order to avoid losing a hardware wallet or private keys. Losing a hardware wallet or keys means losing access to funds. Though the options can make a new investor's head spin, they are essentially the same as gold. Investors can choose paper gold, self-custodied physical gold, or third-party custodied physical gold based on their personal and ideological preferences. Any other conceptualization overcomplicates the matter.

CHAPTER 6

A Look at Common Counterarguments

In my several conversations and writings about Bitcoin, I come across many of the same arguments and concerns. This chapter aims at addressing counterarguments against investing in Bitcoin that the reader may have or never knew existed. Though many are warranted and require technical understanding of concepts such as forking and even quantum computing, others stem from a lack of due diligence. I hope this chapter addresses any final concerns before an investor decides to place at least a small percentage of his or her capital into the asset. I also hope to take a fair view and acknowledge that not all counterarguments can be immediately discounted, though most are overstated. As long as existential threats to the Bitcoin network exist, an investor is taking immense risk in adopting the Bitcoin Standard or investing money that he or she cannot lose. Like any asset, investors must conduct an internal cost–benefit analysis and determine the appropriate allocation accordingly.

"Bitcoin is scarce, but cryptocurrencies are not"

This argument takes two forms. First, it begins with the belief that because Bitcoin is open source, anyone can create another decentralized ledger protocol to dilute the value of Bitcoin. It is based on the idea that one hundred different coins that serve a similar purpose will make Bitcoin worthless. Additionally, someone can fork Bitcoin or make an improvement to the open-source protocol to launch a better coin that will surely surpass Bitcoin in market capitalization. This is verifiably false due to network effects and the fact that most cryptocurrencies are neither anonymous nor decentralized. Litecoin and Bitcoin Cash serve as two examples of proposed Bitcoin upgrades that never reached prominence.

Altcoins oftentimes sell themselves as better versions of Bitcoin or complement cryptocurrencies. Litecoin was created in 2011 by MIT programmer Charlie Lee. The Litecoin network contains 84 million coins to Bitcoin's 21 million. This allows Litecoin to transact more in whole units than fractions and allows for a lower value per coin, which is psychologically more appealing to some investors. Litecoin also runs on a different mining protocol and has greater transaction speed. It takes the Bitcoin network an average of nine minutes for a block to be verified and posted on the blockchain, initially giving it limited use for transactions and scalability. For Litecoin, the transaction time is 2.5 minutes. Litecoin posited itself as the transactional cryptocurrency, while Bitcoin's slow processing time made it the store of value cryptocurrency.

Bitcoin Cash also attempted to supplant Bitcoin. It is the result of a 2017 fork in the Bitcoin network also aimed at improving processing time for transactions and scalability. A hard fork occurs when there is a massive change to the protocol and nodes on the new version no longer accept the old version. The old network continues as usual but a new network, or coin, gets created in the process. Bitcoin Cash is a hard fork of the Bitcoin network that increased the block size from 1MB to 8 MB. As the Bitcoin network grew, it faced issues of processing time and fees to settle transactions when it faced large volumes. Bitcoin Cash could process more transactions per block, thereby freeing the network. Litecoin and Bitcoin Cash were both improvements on the Bitcoin network that made for faster processing so users could make micropayments without slowing the network. Both also retained absolute scarcity. Bitcoin Cash even made the claim that its network met the original intent of Bitcoin's pseudonymous creator, Satoshi Nakamoto, as a digital currency and not a store of value.

If both are clear improvements to the network, why is Bitcoin's market capitalization over 31 times that of Bitcoin Cash and over 49 times that of Litecoin? Why are these two challengers the number 8 and 12 cryptocurrencies respectively, without a realistic avenue to surpass Bitcoin? The answer lies in network effects. Bitcoin won the cryptocurrency race because users agreed that it best met their needs for a digital store of value and medium of exchange. In order for another cryptocurrency to surpass Bitcoin, a majority of users would have to agree that it is better. Not only that, but they would have to collectively leave the Bitcoin network by selling their coins and join the new network by buying those coins.

The cryptocurrency industry has no shortage of talented programmers. There is no hiring or vetting process. Instead, anyone with talent and interest can propose an upgrade. This makes it infinitely more innovative than closed, hierarchical companies. As opposed to collectively joining a new network, Bitcoin solved the scalability problem by adding a layer-two protocol called the lightning network. The lightning network settles transactions instantly off the blockchain, leading to less congestion on the Bitcoin network that allows for more small-scale transactions. Transactions are only updated on the main blockchain after a channel is closed between those transacting. Investors should know that it is far more costly for everyone on the network to simultaneously jump ship to a different network than it is to innovate through a layer-two solution or soft fork. The second incarnation of the previous argument sounds akin to this: "Bitcoin is the Pets.com of blockchain technology. Another, superior coin will enter the market and replace it." Litecoin and Bitcoin Cash prove that the dominant network will find solutions to survive before it relinquishes dominance as it is in the best interest of all users on the network. Before the lightning network, many investors thought Bitcoin would fail due to its scaling and transactional flaws. Though a finished product in itself, Bitcoin's innovative nature allows it to overcome obstacles and constantly improve through soft forks and layer-two solutions such as the lightning network. Those waiting for a superior digital currency do not understand this.

Secondly, some coins have a team of programmers that can alter the code if they deem necessary. Ethereum fits this mold and developers purposefully forked the protocol in 2016 to overcome a hack in a decentralized organization that owned a large percentage of tokens. Many coins, especially those of the Initial Coin Offering (ICO) boom of 2017 have marketing teams, a board of directors, and flexible issuances as determined by its creators. These cryptocurrencies are neither decentralized nor autonomous and make no sense as a Bitcoin substitute. For one, a team of coders controlling one's currency issuance is perhaps a worse substitution than a Central Bank. Secondly, creating a monetary system around a nonmonetary utility token makes as much sense as making Chuck E. Cheese tokens a national currency.

As the next chapter examines, Ethereum and many coins of the ICO boom were never designed to function as mediums of exchange nor stores of value. Much of the verbiage surrounding cryptocurrencies leads to mis-interpretations that this book attempts to resolve. Only a fraction of cryptocurrencies fulfills the purpose of a currency—with the Bitcoin network reigning as the dominant one. The process for achieving network effects for digital assets is more satisficing and innovating around roadblocks than optimizing. Most investors lack the technical knowledge to care about the internal processes of each token, and only care if it best meets their investment criteria.

"It costs too much to buy a coin"

Some investors face a mental barrier when the price per coin reaches several thousands of dollars. Bitcoin is expensive or inexpensive based on the valuation metrics in Chapter 4, not because of its price per coin. Bitcoins are infinitely divisible. The idea that investors must purchase whole coins at a time is simply not accurate. One can invest in Bitcoin with only cents on the dollar, but they will only own a small fraction of a coin. The smallest unit of measure in the Bitcoin space is called the satoshi, or sat. A satoshi is 0.00000001 Bitcoin. In the event that Bitcoin ever reaches reserve currency status, the satoshi will certainly be the unit of measurement due to the astronomical price of an entire coin.

Investors must know that the coin price does not equate to a share price. For example, if the share price of Amazon reaches $4,000, that means $4,000 is the minimum investment to become a shareholder unless a stock split occurs or the investor uses a brokerage account that allows for investing in partial shares. If an investor ever uses this as an argument against investing, he or she is likely facing a mental barrier from an equity-based framework.

"Bitcoin is used by criminals"

The perception of Bitcoin as a tool for money laundering is inextricably linked to its early use case as a pseudonymous currency for illicit online activity. In 2011, Ross Ulbricht created the Silk Road, an anonymous online e-commerce website on the dark web for buying and selling illegal drugs. A former physics major and himself a psychedelic mushroom dealer, Ross's grand vision of Jeff Bezos meets Pablo Escobar ultimately ended in double life imprisonment and 40 years without parole. The Silk Road used Tor software, designed by U.S. Naval Intelligence to obscure an individual's identity when surfing the web. Though potential customers could anonymously surf the Silk Road using Tor, they could not make purchases with a credit or debit card without being traced. Bitcoin's use of a public address posted on the blockchain, as opposed to personally identifiable information through a credit card company or service such as PayPal, created the full anonymity that Ross desired. By the end of 2012, the Silk Road was averaging $1.2 million Bitcoin transactions per month.[1]

The issue Ross faced was that Bitcoin is not anonymous. The blockchain publishes a public, pseudonymous key for every transaction, and authorities have the ability to trace those transactions back to the individual with enough time and effort. For those who hold wallets on centralized exchanges, the exchange can link public keys to individual accounts. Even in the early days of Bitcoin, the United States Federal Bureau of Investigation (FBI) made Silk Road related arrests on a monthly basis.[2] Bitcoin's use as a perfectly anonymous currency for criminals is highly exaggerated. For legal activities where anonymity is desired, such as online gambling, Bitcoin surely has its use case. However, for illicit activities such as terrorist financing, ransomware, and drug dealing, having every transaction posted on the blockchain with a public key serves as a major disadvantage. Blockchain monitoring companies such as ComplyAdvantage and Elliptic work hand-in-hand with authorities to monitor cryptocurrency transactions and link them to criminal activity.

The ultimate irony behind the claim that Bitcoin is used for money laundering is the fact criminals use cash and megabanks far more often than Bitcoin. Meanwhile, governments and Wall Street are usually among the first to claim that Bitcoin is for criminals. According to a crypto crime report by Chainalysis that oversaw roughly $1 trillion worth of Bitcoin transactions each year since 2017, only 0.34 percent of transactions in 2020 were associated with illicit activity.[3] The majority of illicit activities involve scams, ransomware, or darknet matters similar to the old Silk Road in spite of crackdowns. That equates to $5 billion of illicit crypto-related activities a year. Meanwhile, according to the United Nations Office on Drugs and Crime, criminals use cash to launder between

$800 billion and $2 trillion annually—which equates between 2 and 5 percent of global GDP. Cash and cash businesses will always be the primary method for criminals to launder money. Meanwhile, big money international criminals prefer using Wall Street banks. A study conducted by the International Consortium of Investigative Journalists (ICIJ) concluded that JPMorgan, HSBC, Standard Chartered Bank, Deutsche Bank, and Bank of New York Mellon all continued laundering funds for high-net worth criminals even after fines and warnings from the U.S. Department of Justice. A short list of clients includes a corrupt vice-president of the Democratic Republic of Congo, a Venezuelan energy mogul whose embezzlement contributed to nationwide blackouts, and an Iranian gold trader evading sanctions.[4]

The early use case of Bitcoin as a pseudonymous currency used in online drug trafficking will always give it a negative perception. Statistically, cash is used far more often for money laundering because it is more anonymous. Bitcoin publishes a public key to the blockchain that can help authorities trace funds back to individuals. While the world focuses on the narrative of Bitcoin as a money laundering device, megabanks benefit from toothless Treasury officials and willfully ignorant internal compliance departments. In 2011, JP Morgan Chase faced an $88.3 million fine to settle a case of knowingly violating economic sanctions against Iran. In 2014, it made $500 million in fees and interest from Bernie Madoff alone.

"I believe in blockchain, just not Bitcoin"

I believe this stems from a lack of understanding of both blockchain and Bitcoin. Blockchain itself is much slower and expensive than centralized solutions. The only advantage of using blockchain is to eliminate a third party between transactions, whether monetary or otherwise. It can only do this through a decentralized token native to the blockchain and a consensus mechanism such as proof-of-work to validate authenticity and prevent double spending. For Bitcoin, a distributed ledger based on proof-of-work is energy- and time-intensive. A centralized database such as Visa can process 65,000 transactions per second. The Bitcoin network is only capable of processing four transactions per second, hence the need for layer-two solutions such as the lightning network.

Additionally, Bitcoin mining and transactions currently consume over 120 terawatt-hours of electricity per year. This equates to 0.28 percent of all global electricity and more than medium-sized countries such as Switzerland, Ireland, and Israel. A single Bitcoin transaction consumes 741 kilowatt-hours of electricity. By comparison, 100,000 Visa transactions consumes 149 kilowatt-hours. Though some projects use proof-of-stake to minimize electricity use, the benefits of decentralization must far outweigh the costs in time and energy in order to create a successful blockchain project. Detractors commonly use the argument of migrating all information such as medical records or personal records onto the blockchain for security purposes. If the bank or hospital is the trusted third party that owns the records regardless, migrating to the blockchain is just an extra, inefficient step in most cases. They would be much better off bolstering their current database security measures.

The only truly successful use cases of blockchain technology are Bitcoin and Ethereum. Ethereum is a programmable blockchain that uses self-executing smart contracts. Think of this as an IF, THEN statement in basic code. When the IF event occurs, the contract executes the THEN portion of the statement. It requires no legal, financial, or medical intermediary. Though the premise seems simple, individuals can build entire subnetworks on the Ethereum platform. In fact, roughly 90 percent of Altcoins are built on the Ethereum protocol. Ethereum allows for peer-to-peer borrowing and lending, fundraising, gaming, stablecoins, fractional real estate ownership, insurance payments, supply chain management, and more. It is the application token of blockchain technology. The Ethereum blockchain is a solution still seeking problems to solve and has taken a life of its own in recent years.

Bitcoin, meanwhile, serves the fundamental purpose of transferring value on the blockchain. Why would someone want to transfer value in a peer-to-peer manner? Banks, payment companies such as Visa, money transfer companies such as Western Union, and even title companies charge time and fees by being the third party between value transactions. These companies also have the ability to deny transactions. Additionally, Bitcoin's sound and immutable monetary policy makes it a safe haven from capital controls, hyperinflating currencies, or steadily inflating currencies. It is the only transactional currency that cannot possibly be debased. Lastly, because it is peer-to-peer and not connected to the legacy financial system, any Bitcoin held in cold storage is sovereign. In 2018, Greek officials seized over 105,000 bank accounts for alleged tax evasion. Though the owners of these accounts committed a crime, the fact that governments have the ability to seize your assets concerns some. A market always existed for a decentralized hard currency and blockchain enabled it by disintermediating banks and governments from money. As governments around the world continue to debase their currencies to stimulate in a low-rate environment, that market for Bitcoin will grow. Immutable money warrants the additional processing time and energy required.

Anyone who states that they believe in blockchain technology but not Bitcoin understands neither. Blockchain is a disintermediary technology with limited applications. It eliminates central authority but adds slower processing time and high energy costs because it requires a verification mechanism—proof-of-work algorithm for Bitcoin and the less energy-intensive proof-of-stake for Ethereum. Transferring value without a bank or government constitutes the best possible application of blockchain. Second would be executing contracts without a central authority to mediate the contract, though it has diverse implications and use cases. The financial infrastructure has seen little technological innovation in recent decades. Individuals can conduct a frictionless, face-to-face call from different continents, but sending value via international wire transfer takes several business days. The system was ripe for innovation. Bitcoin and Ethereum exposed inefficiencies that most individuals did not know existed.

"Bitcoin consumes too much energy"

Bitcoin mining is an energy-intensive business. Ethereum began transitioning from proof-of-work to proof-of-stake with Ethereum 2.0 to decrease energy consumption, though at a cost that will be explored later in this book. The high energy consumption from Bitcoin mining derives from the processing power used by miners in solving the computational puzzle to verify blocks. Miners would have to sell Bitcoin in order to cover operating costs from electricity usage and equipment. Proof-of-stake attributes mining power in direct proportion to the number of coins held, not by computational power and energy. If one agrees to stake coins for an indeterminable amount of time, one is rewarded with additional coins. Ethereum is a much more experimental and fluid project than Bitcoin with disparate applications and constant upgrades. Arguably, proof-of-stake makes Ethereum much less egalitarian. Despite proof-of-stake's proposed advantages in terms of energy, proof-of-work is proven to correctly mix the incentives between miners and investors.

As an energy-intensive business, some detractors will claim that Bitcoin harms the environment by releasing carbon emissions from its energy usage. They will also claim that such high energy usage is not warranted for a speculative financial asset. First, Bitcoin mining operations are only profitable in areas with low energy costs. In Sichuan, China, home to the second largest Bitcoin mining operation in the world, an overcapacity of hydropower provides roughly 75 GW of power annually, which is double the requirement of the city's power grid.[5] This readily available excess energy supply made Sichuan a perfect candidate for a Bitcoin mining operation. Entrepreneurs can also repurpose failing energy sources for Bitcoin mining, such as the Alcoa aluminum smelting factory in upstate New York.

Bitcoin mining tends to occur in areas with excess capacity of energy because it provides miners with a competitive advantage through less operating costs. Bitcoin will not drive-up energy costs in the average city or town because it remains relegated to rural, energy-efficient areas such as Sichuan and upstate New York. Additionally, 39 percent of all Bitcoin mining operations rely on renewable energy according to a 2020 report, with 74 percent of mining operations using renewables as part of their energy mix.[6] According to the International Energy Agency (IEA), 28 percent of the world's energy usage relies on renewable sources. Bitcoin mining operations are much greener than the global average.

More importantly, at 120 terawatt-hours compared to global annual production of 160,000 terawatt-hours of energy, the Bitcoin network currently consumes 0.075 percent of global energy at the time of this writing. As Microstrategy's Michael Saylor points out, 50,000 terawatt-hours of the 160,000 is considered waste. Bitcoin consumes 0.25 percent of wasted energy. These figures make complaints of Bitcoin's energy consumption silly by comparison. The truth is, any amount of electricity will be too much for most Bitcoin detractors. For those who use Bitcoin for remittance payments to their families or for monetary sovereignty in the face of capital controls, hyperinflating currencies, or surreptitious taxation through a policy of inflation, this energy consumption is well worth it.

Additionally, as energy sources such as solar and hydropower become more efficient and coal plants more expensive, renewable energy will undoubtedly grow in relative market size. According to a study by Carbon Tracker in 2018, 42 percent of the world's coal plants are operating at a loss. Meanwhile, Swanson's Law states that the price of solar energy drops roughly 20 percent when the shipped volume of solar cells doubles, equating to a price drop of 75 percent every 10 years. In the near future, renewable energy sources such as solar and wind will be more efficient and less expensive than coal, which has high exploration and maintenance costs. I do not worry about the carbon emission argument from detractors because Bitcoin is relegated to energy-efficient areas, relies heavily on green energy, and the shift to renewable energy is economically and politically inevitable. Solar power is set to be more cost efficient than coal by the year 2030.

The second claim is that energy usage to power a speculative financial asset is wasteful and unproductive. Bitcoin and cryptocurrencies are not just financial assets, but an entire fledgling alternative financial industry that employs miners, investors, lawmakers, and more. Repurposing the Alcoa mine in New York alone created 150 jobs.[7] A 2020 search query study conducted by Bitcoin.com found roughly 8,000 crypto- and blockchain-related job openings. Common positions include software engineers, program managers, community managers, and compliance officers. Energy is not being funneled to a speculative asset, but a fledgling industry that continues to grow.

In the ultimate sign of an industry being born, college students are demanding Bitcoin- and blockchain-related curriculum. The MBA to crypto pipeline is only in its infancy with MBA programs recently rolling out crypto-related curriculum. Stanford's first cryptocurrency class in 2018 was a grass roots movement led by student Itamar Orr and a group of classmates noticing Silicon Valley's interest. Additionally, trends in MBA employment demonstrates a shifting nexus of hiring from Wall Street to Silicon Valley and crypto. For example, 2007 graduates of Stanford went on to begin finance careers 38 percent of the time compared to

12 percent for technology-related careers. In 2017, those figures changed to 24 percent finance and 25 percent technology.[8] This trend itself foretold of the rise of big tech and FAANG stocks. As large Silicon Valley venture capital firms continue plowing into crypto, such as Andreessen Horowitz's $865 million worth of investments in crypto funds, and continue being more attractive to MBA graduates over traditional finance, crypto will see more institutional buy-in and will become mainstream in even MBA education. Educational involvement gives more credence to the idea that this is a fledgling industry, not just a singular asset.

Both Wall Street and Silicon Valley are competing for market share in the ongoing crypto boom, with other cities such as the San Francisco, Wyoming, and Miami all vying for the business that it brings. The city of Miami even uploaded the Bitcoin white paper to its municipal website in 2021, with Mayor Francis Suarez promising to turn the city into a hub for crypto innovation. Bitcoin investing, mining, lending, and blockchain applications are all part of a greater industry. Hysteria regarding Bitcoin's energy consumption is overblown—especially when compared to its societal benefits. Furthermore, Bitcoin's energy consumption takes advantage of low-cost energy sources, relies largely in large part on green energy, and will continue to do so as it inevitably becomes more economically advantageous. Lastly, that energy is not just powering a speculative asset, but an entire industry that cities and traditional universities around the world are trying to co-opt.

"Bitcoin has no intrinsic value"

I hope that Chapter 4 settled this counterargument, but it bears repeating. Bitcoin's value derives from demand in the face of scarcity. A 2016 report commissioned by Art Basel and UBS Global estimated the value of the global collectible art market to be $56.6 billion.[9] Original paintings contain scarcity even though they can be replicated indefinitely online and in print. I liken this aspect to Bitcoin versus Altcoins. Bitcoin replicas exist, but users agree that Bitcoin is the best autonomous and decentralized monetary network. The only utility of art involves looking at it as a decoration—though no one would claim that it has no value despite its lack of utility. Collectible art, cars, baseball cards, and the like, derive most of their value from scarcity. However, due to the subjectivity and changing tastes of collectors, even collectible items have a regular flow of recently determined collectibles. At 21 million, Bitcoin is the only asset as scarce as time. It is programmed scarcity. Scarce items that hold value have a great premium with today's monetary economics.

Bitcoin also has utility value as a peer-to-peer payment mechanism that avoids the negative effects of sending money via trusted third parties. Bitcoin sees significant demand from this direction as well. Shares in Visa stock involve ownership in that corporation. Owning Bitcoin makes you a partial owner of the most dominant decentralized monetary network. Similar to commodities and dissimilar to financial assets, value is based solely on supply and demand. Consistent demand and a four-year halving cycle leads to increasing price. In a reflexive loop, increasing price brings more attention and demand. My response to the question of intrinsic value usually involves follow-on questions. Why does an original Van Gogh painting have value? Why do shares in Visa have value? Why has gold out-performed Berkshire Hathaway since 2001? Investors who use a financial asset valuation framework to a commodity will remain in the dark.

"Governments will ban Bitcoin if it becomes too successful"

I saved what I believe to be the most legitimate Bitcoin counterarguments for last. First, governments cannot ban Bitcoin because it is completely decentralized. Bitcoin will exist as long as one server in the world runs a full node and as long as the Internet exists. Even then, one can send Bitcoins via radio waves. However, an argument exists for governments denying Bitcoin transactions and purchases on major exchanges or by private companies. This will undoubtedly affect the price though the network will continue to exist. Bitcoin's market capitalization is much too small for governments to concern themselves over at the current moment. However, current trends such Bitcoin-populism will lead to more government scrutiny while trends such as institutional entrenchment will lead to less.

At a macro scale, printing and injecting money to alleviate economic woes creates moral hazard and maintains inefficient companies at the expense of innovation. Keeping borrowing costs below their free market levels also provides advantages to those large institutions with access to capital. In a free market, the marginal product of capital determines interest rates. In a neo-Keynesian economy, central planners determine the appropriate level of interest to meet their goals of increasing economic activity and employment. Pushing the cost of capital downward to alleviate economic weakness is a short-sighted solution to a structural problem. Liquidity injections even more so. Following the 2008 financial crisis, Citigroup, Bank of America, JP Morgan Chase, Goldman Sachs, and Morgan Stanley received a combined $135 billion in bailouts.[10] This book does not intend to make normative statements about bailouts but only points it out as a public example of how policy choices have fueled national discontent. In fact, for the sake of argument, I will assume the best-case scenario. Policy makers' quick action averted large-scale human suffering in 2008 and the nation and economy are better off for it.

The moral hazard of the bailouts involves using public funds to cushion the balance sheets of banks at the epicenter of the subprime mortgage crisis. The average individual who took excess risk was forced to reap what they sow. Today's liquidity injections and policy of inflation bolster financial assets and alleviate debtors at a time when wages have remained stagnant since the 1970s. It benefits asset holders and debtors while taxing wage earners and savers. In essence, it makes the rich, richer and the poor, poorer. Much of the developed world has this same policy. Rates at the zero bound lead to accelerated money printing, which widens the wealth gap. I believe this is the source of 21st-century global populism. Black Lives Matter protests, storming the Capitol building, and antilockdown protests are all symptoms of a greater discontent. Though the average person lays blame to an institution, race, culture, country, or political party, I believe the seed of their discontent is a financial system that provides exorbitant privilege to banks, corporations, and governments because they have access to both cheap capital and public funds.

Since 1983, this system has led to a halving of the middle class in terms of their share in U.S. aggregate wealth, and a 19 percent rise of those considered upper income according to Pew Research.[11] Bitcoin markets itself as a parallel financial system outside the control of governments and banks. In fact, nearly every technological breakthrough in mankind has marketed itself as a cure for societies' cultural and moral woes. In 1922, the director of the Radio Corporation of America had this to say about radio: "whatever he most desires… the radio telephone will supply it. We can be certain that a national cultural appreciation will result… the people's University of the Air will have a greater student body than all of our universities put together."[12] Advocates will oftentimes use a moralistic argument and offer Bitcoin as a way to "opt out" of the current financial system. Though the merits of that argument are up for discussion, it proves salient during eras of discontent.

The Wall Street versus Main Street debate of 2008 was reopened in 2021 when users of a Reddit subforum, noting that short interest in GameStop had exceeded 100 percent of available shares, piled into the stock to create a massive short squeeze that sent the price from $2.57 a share to nearly $500. The popular retail brokerage app Robinhood, responded by halting buy orders on the stock, citing it needed to "protect our firm and our customers," not liquidity issues in posting collateral at clearing houses as many suspected. Many believe that it halted buy orders so that hedge funds could get out of their short positions and lick their wounds. Robinhood disclosures show that it sells customers' trading information to hedge funds such as Citadel owned by Ken Griffin. Melvin Capital, the short-selling hedge fund that lost billions in the short squeeze, is owned by Citadel. Along with Steve Cohen's Point72 hedge fund, Citadel was forced to infuse Melvin with $3 billion to shore up finances following the events.

Again, whether Robinhood's decision truly was a liquidity issue that the CEO did not wish to disclose, or if they halted buying to help their Wall Street clients is beside the point. Personally, I believe that inability to post collateral with prime brokers certainly played a role in the events that ensued. However, perception is reality. These events added fuel to the fire behind the idea that the financial system is corrupt and favors the few at the expense of the many. For Bitcoin traditionalists, this is what Bitcoin was made for. I believe these disgruntled traders are one step away from angrily ditching traditional finance entirely and migrating to decentralized digital assets.

As previously stated, Bitcoin's market capitalization is much too small for most regulators to concern themselves over. However, recent events demonstrate that Bitcoin strikes a populist chord. Actions in El Salvador prove that entire countries can now choose to "opt out" of the dollar centric international order. What if Bitcoin becomes the outlet for current

global populist sentiment? What if citizens vote with their wallets by joining a parallel financial system and leaving the traditional financial system
of debt, inflation, dollars, stocks, and bonds? Marketing Bitcoin as outside of government control is one thing, marketing it as antiestablishment
is another. One invites a co-opt from traditional finance that can lead to
its adoption as an institutional asset. The other invites heavy handed regulation. Bitcoin's future most likely lies in the middle with institutional
adoption accompanied by increased regulation.

Despite the concerning covenant being made between Bitcoin and
disgruntled populists, I still believe that governments are more likely to
co-opt than combat Bitcoin because we are currently seeing massive traditional financial entrenchment. As more powerful individuals and institutions allocate a portion of their portfolios to Bitcoin, governments will
become less combative. Additionally, a ban is complicated by the fact
that Bitcoin is legal tender in one country and will become legal tender
in more. Due to the western world's acceptance thus far, examples of
institutional interest grow on a monthly basis. Some current examples
include Fidelity Digital Assets for institutional investors, Visa offering a
Bitcoin rewards card, PayPal and CashApp allowing Bitcoin transactions,
Microsoft Identity on the Bitcoin network, MassMutual Insurance portfolio adding Bitcoin, Goldman Sachs and JP Morgan creating cryptocurrency trading desks and providing banking services to major exchanges,
hedge funds such as Skybridge Capital adding Bitcoin, and municipal
governments inviting the industry to their jurisdictions for the economic
benefits. The list goes on. Additionally, cryptocurrency exchanges such
as Coinbase and Gemini, crypto-insurance companies such as Evertas,
Bitcoin lending options such as BlockFi, and rewards credit cards such as
the Fold Card all show that crypto companies also have significant financial power already. Making the industry illegal or highly regulated in one
fell swoop will upset both legacy finance and the new finance crowd at
this point. It will also lead to a migration of capital as the Chinese mining
example will illustrate later in this chapter. The time to ban Bitcoin was
in its infancy. With such institutional and international entrenchment,
I believe a complete ban is off the table.

Contrary to the idea that governments would be combative to a technology that challenges their monopoly on money, the opposite seems to be
occurring with the international rollout of Central Bank Digital Currencies

(CBDCs). Governments and traditional finance are actually embracing decentralized currencies despite their preferential treatment with populists and anarcho-capitalists because they make money in doing so and co-opting it is less costly than stopping it from a game theory perspective. As mentioned in previous chapters, a ban would require international coordination because one country's loss is another country's gain. The country's crypto-economy will shift to whichever country has the more friendly regulation. We are currently witnessing this at the Federal level in the United States with states such as Florida and Texas attracting those in the crypto-industry with friendlier policies. Not only does entrenchment make a ban unlikely, but a ban is simply too difficult to execute.

"Quantum computing will hack the Bitcoin network"

Quantum computers use the concepts of superposition and entanglement to create exponentially larger processing power compared to regular computing systems. Superposition allows quantum computers to be in multiple states simultaneously. While regular systems compute and store information in binary bits of 0 or 1, quantum systems use quibits that can be both states at the same time. Additionally, because quibits can be in the same state through entanglement, adding extra bits to a quantum computer leads to exponentially greater processing power. With a regular system, doubling the bits equals doubling processing power. With exponentially larger processing power, seemingly impossible problems become solvable. One of which, hypothetically, includes Bitcoin cryptography.

Bitcoin uses cryptography in both the proof-of-work algorithm and in creating public keys. The Secure Hash Algorithm 256 (SHA-256) is the cryptographic function that must be solved by miners to create Bitcoin. Quantum computing threatens the mining industry because it has exponentially greater processing power that can solve the algorithm faster and mine all future available Bitcoin before regular competitors. More importantly, sufficiently high quantum computing could derive a private key from its corresponding public key, thus falsifying any digital signatures and stealing coins. A Bitcoin private key is a randomly generated 256-bit alphanumerical combination used in digital signatures to verify transactions. When a private key is put through the Elliptic Curve

Digital Signature Algorithm (ECDSA), it creates a corresponding public key. There is a mathematical relationship between public and private keys, though only the public key gets posted on the blockchain while the private key validates transactions. Though technically possible, reverse engineering a public key to derive a private key takes an astronomical amount of computing power that current computers cannot achieve.

Quantum supercomputers are nowhere near proficient enough to hack either algorithm. Estimates show that cracking Bitcoin cryptography would require at least 1,500 quibits according to most sources. The closest computer in existence today is Google's 53 quibit supercomputer. However, the supercomputer checks outputs from a quantum random number generator. It has no applications and poses no threat to the network. It took nearly 50 years since the introduction of quantum computing to achieve this feat. Creating a 1,500 quibit supercomputer capable of reverse engineering cryptography would be a massive undertaking and is in all probability a century or more away. Quantum computing is unlikely to threaten the Bitcoin network in my lifetime. Even when it does, solutions still exist to keep the network alive.

Soft forks and layer-two solutions can both prevent quantum computers from hacking the Bitcoin network. As opposed to a hard fork that creates two different protocols and thus an entirely new coin, a soft fork constitutes a minor upgrade to the network that old nodes accept as legitimate. Hard forks constitute major, noncompatible changes to the protocol. Nine hard forks have occurred from the original Bitcoin protocol. Most have become obsolete and none have come close to surpassing the original protocol in market capitalization. Meanwhile, the Bitcoin network has accepted 26 soft-forks from different developers. Anyone can propose a "Bitcoin Improvement Proposal" on the Bitcoin GitHub site—a website for community software projects. It first gets screened and approved by an editor. Then, 95 percent of the last 2,016 miners must approve the upgrade as legitimate. Lastly, all miners must update their software. The supermajority required in Bitcoin governance means that upgrading the network is difficult but not impossible. One example of a soft fork involved adopting the segregated witness (SegWit) update in 2017, which increased the block limit from one to four in order to improve transaction processing time.

Quantum computing threatens the security of any system that uses cryptography. Most online systems that involve transactions, such as online banking and e-commerce, rely on public key cryptography that is less secure than Bitcoin. Therefore, quantum computing could first hack login information from a bank or credit card information from an e-commerce website before taking one's Bitcoin. A quantum-resistant public key cryptography system will be developed in due time because a failure to do so will compromise every piece of secure information on the Internet. Bitcoin will adopt it through a soft fork or through a second layer security solution. Additionally, Bitcoin is already quantum-resistant if one takes the proper measures—and not just through cold storage. In order for a hacker to access your Bitcoin, they must have your private key and public key. The public key also serves as the address. A hacker will only see your public address as it becomes posted to the blockchain after a transaction. If you move your Bitcoin to a new address after a transaction, a hacker cannot access them, even with a quantum supercomputer.

In summation, quantum computing is in all likelihood a century or more away before threatening the Bitcoin network. Even then, it equally threatens traditional banking and e-commerce. We will have cybersecurity upgrades before allowing quantum computing to break the Internet. Bitcoin could easily adopt these through a soft fork or layer-two solution. Though a legitimate threat given the current state of the network, Bitcoin developers and global cybersecurity experts have decades to react. The technology to protect these networks does not exist yet because the technology to attack them has yet to reach any meaningful milestones.

"Derivatives markets will keep Bitcoin's price suppressed"

A derivative is a financial contract whose price is anchored to a specific asset. Traders oftentimes use derivatives to hedge risk exposure or gain access to otherwise unavailable assets. Types of financial derivatives include futures, options, swaps, and forward contracts. Traders can use derivatives to get exposure to stocks, bonds, currencies, commodities, and interest rates. Because the derivatives user does not own the underlying asset, derivatives is a popular strategy among traders and hedge funds, not long-term investors.

On October 31, 2017, the Chicago Board Options Exchange (CBOE) launched a futures contract based on Bitcoin. This occurred three years after the decision by the Commodity Futures Trading Commission (CFTC) to define Bitcoin as a commodity according to the Commodity Exchange Act. District courts upheld the CFTC's decision to treat cryptocurrencies as commodities in multiple public lawsuits, lending credence to its legitimacy and providing enough regulation for more commodities exchanges to get involved. After increased pressure from institutional funds, the Chicago Mercantile Exchange (CME), the largest options and futures contracts exchange in the world, announced that it too would begin Bitcoin futures trading in December 2017. In another milestone, the CFTC approved physical delivery of Bitcoin as opposed to cash-settled contracts for the LedgerX derivatives exchange and clearinghouse in June 2019, making it the first fully collateralized futures exchange. Most investors see futures trading as the first of several institutional floodgates that will lead to upward price action. The largest and most liquid oil futures contracts, West Texas Intermediate Crude, trades 1.2 million contracts per day. Additionally, those with high Bitcoin exposure such as miners can purchase long-term put options to hedge their exposure, giving it practical application to the industry.

While most see the introduction of Bitcoin derivatives as a positive, others claim that the ability to short an asset without owning a claim to the underlying in a process called naked short selling means large institutions can keep the price of Bitcoin perpetually suppressed. Critics blame derivatives for the housing market collapse in 2008, as mortgage-backed securities are in fact a derivative on an underlying mortgage bundle. A popular belief among gold investors is that the gold market is manipulated downward through derivative contracts in a way reminiscent of the 1960s London Gold Pool, where global Central Banks collectively bought and sold gold on the open market to maintain the $35/oz dollar for gold convertibility. In the 1960s, the incentives lay in maintaining the Bretton Woods system of dollar convertibility and preventing runs on the gold reserves of the United States. Today, some gold investors claim that governments and banks have the incentive of preventing runs on the dollar and keeping investable assets within the financial system as opposed to a monetary asset. I believe the claims are false, but not entirely unwarranted.

The first method of suppressing price involves naked short selling, arguably witnessed in the 2021 events involving GameStop. Naked shorting is the illegal practice of short selling without ever having the asset, or short selling an asset that does not exist. Hedge funds and individual traders were able to get 140 percent short on GameStop. In other words, there was more short pressure than available shares. While those with options expertise will claim that lending out borrowed shares more than once can lead to this dynamic, the fact that traders shorted more than the available float remains. The second method involves "spoofing," the act of placing large trade orders with the intent of canceling them before execution. Algorithmic trading platforms will buy or sell in advance of the fake trade, ultimately playing into the hands of the original trader with a preexisting trade. The CFTC forced J.P. Morgan to pay $920 million in fines and restitution after it determined that "between 2008 and 2016, JPMorgan engaged in a pattern of manipulation in the precious metals futures and U.S. Treasury futures market."[13]

Precious metals manipulation occurs, but to what extent? I believe cries of foul play are overstated. Short interest is publicly available data. Similar to GameStop in 2021, high short interest met with more demand creates short squeezes that lead to skyrocketing price action. Any high volume naked short squeezing will likely be short-lived. Additionally, spoofing may work for short-term price action but I do not believe that headfaking algorithmic traders can lead to sustained bull and bear markets. Meanwhile, cries of Central Bank and investment bank collusion to suppress gold prices lie in the realm of conspiracy theory. Since 2000, gold has outperformed the S&P 500 by over 359 percent due to a huge rally at the turn of the millennia. Since 2010, it has underperformed by 194 percent and performed on par in the last two years. If global Central Banks and investment banks are colluding to keep the price of gold suppressed, my contention is that they are doing a terrible job of it. Investors worried that financialization of Bitcoin will lead to manipulation through derivatives usually believe in an overstated gold manipulation narrative.

"China owns too much of the Bitcoin network"

At the time of this writing, sixty-five percent of the Bitcoin mining pool, as measured by the hash rate, exists in China.[14] This causes some detractors to argue against Bitcoin on a geostrategic basis. In addition to China's high hash rate, Russia owns 6.9 percent compared to 7.2 percent in the United States. The argument goes that nefarious global actors use Bitcoin as a means to acquire dollars on the open market. In addition to financing rogue nations, miners can ban together to successfully complete a 51 percent attack on the Bitcoin network and come away with multiple hundreds of billions—largely from U.S. traders and investors. While most of the mining capacity lies in China, most of the trading volume comes from the United States at 38 percent compared to China's 4.95 percent.[15] I believe this argument assumes that Bitcoin mining rigs in China are state-owned enterprises or that China has an interest in subverting the dollar's hegemony through Bitcoin. In fact, China's hostility toward Bitcoin mining has led to a flight of capital to cheap energy sources without antagonistic policies. A continued hostile stance will lead to continued capital flight. This counterargument also does not take into account the game theory that explains why the successful orchestrators of a 51 percent attack would essentially come away with less than that if they continued their business as usual.

Why does Bitcoin investing take place primarily in the United States while Bitcoin mining is primarily done in China, with Russia behind the United States as the third largest Bitcoin miner in the world? Bitcoin is a global phenomenon and a masterclass in free market economics. China has an overcapacity of energy and the United States an overcapacity of capital. Bitcoin mining and investing serves as an outlet for both. As previously mentioned, the competitive advantage in terms of mining goes to those with cheap energy costs. Russia's income from natural resources such as oil and natural gas are 15 percent of GDP. For the United States, that number is 0.71 percent. China achieved a GDP growth rate above 7 percent between 1991 and 2015 largely on a sleight of hand of credit and infrastructure expansion that led to vast energy overcapacity. In addition to largely unnecessary power infrastructure projects such as Sichuan's hydroelectric plant, China's coal-powered plants ran at less than 50 percent capacity on average in 2019. China was forced to cancel three renewable energy projects in 2019 "amid concerns of overcapacity and a $20 billion payment backlog."[16] In a global free market, China's energy overcapacity from mismanaged growth projects made it an ideal candidate for Bitcoin mining. As the wealthiest nation in the world, the United States has the capital to invest in Bitcoin.

The idea that nefarious states mine Bitcoin in their jurisdictions and trade them for dollars is simply not true because these mining operations are not state-owned enterprises. In fact, China is one of the least Bitcoin-friendly nations in the world. Initial Coin Offerings, accepting Bitcoin as legal tender, and local Chinese Bitcoin exchanges have been banned since 2017. In April of 2019, the National Development and Reform Commission (NDRC) submitted a draft to illegalize "virtual currency mining, such as the production process of Bitcoin."[17] Though never approved, Bitcoin hash rates in China decreased by 10 percent in the year and a half since the legislation proposal. It has decreased 15 percent from its high of 80 percent of the total hash rate in 2018. To account for the drop in China, shares of the mining pool have increased by 4.75 percent in Kazakhstan, 3.18 percent in the United States, and 1.12 percent in Malaysia since Q3 2019. China's share of the mining pool continues decreasing on a quarterly basis as its haphazard and hostile regulatory measures causes global miners to find cheap energy elsewhere.

Bitcoin follows the same dynamics as goods in China or Mexico being produced cheaply due to low labor costs and sold to western consumers due to high demand, only substituting labor with energy costs. Treating it as a Chinese conspiracy to generate dollars through mining is undoubtedly false. Additionally, it should be clear by now that the United States is not financing the Chinese Communist Party (CCP) by purchasing Bitcoin on the open market because the CCP has nothing to do with these miners. Investors do not have to take my word for it. The greatest evidence lies in the 15 percent drop in China's hash rate since its initial hard stance on crypto. The CCP is completely antagonistic toward Bitcoin to its own detriment. Losing a profitable industry that provides an outlet to its excess energy capacity is perhaps one of the greatest own goals in economic history. Even while nations with cheap energy profit by mining Bitcoin, the U.S. profits by purchasing and owning most of it though companies such as Grayscale Investment Trust, Coinbase, CashApp, Microstrategies, crypto hedge funds, and the like. Its growing interest in the asset also leads to a growing share of the mining pool.

The second contention to China's role in the mining industry is the idea that independent Chinese miners could band together to conduct a 51 percent attack on the network. A 51 percent attack can occur when one actor has 51 percent or more of the hash rate. This actor could spend a Bitcoin while simultaneously mining a fraudulent fork of the blockchain with another transaction of the same Bitcoin. A 51 percent attack gives the actor the ability to double spend coins, not steal coins or manipulate certain immutable aspects of the blockchain. I believe using a lens of game theory to assess possibilities such as these demonstrates their unlikeliness. First, mining is a profitable industry because one achieves cash flows in an appreciating currency that easily covers operating costs in a depreciating currency. The status quo is to remain a benevolent actor and remain very profitable. Banding together for a 51 percent attack is difficult to achieve in the first place. Even if it occurs because miners decided to or because the CCP had a change of heart and nationalized all mining operations, allowing one actor to double spend their coins destroys the integrity of the network and the purpose behind Bitcoin. A malevolent actor attacks the network for economic gain in the ability to double spend coins, but destroys the network in the process and crashes the price. The actor gains the ability to double spend a coin that it made worthless. I borrowed this colorful analogy from Sam Harris, a popular podcast host and neuroscientist. If being harsh on Bitcoin to the detriment of your economy constitutes an own goal, attacking the network for economic gain only to destroy it and leave your coins worthless is a Lionel Messi-style bicycle kick into your own goal. All actors involved in the network have more incentive to maintain the network than to attack it. Additionally, given that China's share in the mining pool continues to decrease year-over-year, the CCP nationalizing Chinese miner's argument becomes weaker by the day.

The China model demonstrates what not to do when threatened by a decentralized, sovereign currency. All attempts to illegalize or overregulate its Bitcoin mining operations have caused miners to leave for Kazakhstan and Malaysia. Meanwhile, treating it as any other industry or asset would have solved its issues of excess energy capacity and benefited the government through taxation. Lastly and very importantly, investors should know that 88 percent of Bitcoin are already mined and in circulation. By the time quantum computing threatens to break the SHA-56 algorithm or coerced miners join forces to conduct a 51 percent attack, there will likely be little to no Bitcoin left to mine. Additionally, any competitive advantage in mining will be short-lived as much of the profits have been made. The true advantage lies in the industries surrounding the asset itself which, unlike mining, have no shelf life. In developing these industries, the competitive advantage lies in capital-intensive geographies such as the west.

Conclusion

Counterarguments against Bitcoin lie on the spectrum of completely erroneous to legitimate threats. An investor who claims that the price of a Bitcoin is too high simply does not understand the asset. While concerns regarding quantum computing or China's geostrategic role in mining have more credence, I hope to have provided ample evidence to prove that they pose an overstated existential threat to the network. Regardless, investors must understand the different risks that exist.

By this point, investors should have a far more in-depth understanding of Bitcoin as an asset, its role in portfolio management, its role in international economics, and even methods to determine objective and subjective value. It is a truly macro asset that has technological, geopolitical, and even social implications. The rest of the book focuses on the rest of the cryptocurrency ecosystem—beginning with Ethereum. It uses an abbreviated version of the Bitcoin framework that answers what they are, how they fit into a portfolio, and how to value them—all the while uncovering important technical aspects that every potential crypto investor should know.

CHAPTER 7

On Ethereum and Altcoins

Peruse crypto-Twitter for any reasonable amount of time and one will quickly notice the tribalism that exists within Bitcoin and Ethereum crowds. The Bitcoin tribe will claim that "ETH is not money." Ethereum does not have a supply limit and the current number of coins in circulation can only be approximated. The approximation results from Ethereum's use of an account model as opposed to Bitcoin's unspent transaction output (UTXO) model that verifies every transaction. Though not exact, an account-based transaction model better supports the application of smart contracts. Due to this, hard money enthusiasts dismiss Ethereum as no better than fiat currency. When asked about the total Ethereum supply, Vitalik Buterin, cofounder of Ethereum, claimed that "we roughly know what it is according to protocol rules."[1] As the Bitcoin crowd continued to pressure Buterin based on this statement, he refuted claims that he and his cofounders are "inflationist technocrats" when, in June 2020, he pointed out that Ethereum's supply was 40 million coins less than expected from estimates in the original whitepaper published in 2013.[2]

Ethereum proponents point out that the entire Decentralized Finance (DeFi) trend interrupting traditional banking and payment rails is in fact built on the Ethereum network. For early adopters, Bitcoin's core philosophy has a libertarian, anti-establishment tilt. These adopters praise anything that forces governments and large institutions to downsize or anything that imposes more responsibility on what they see as reckless and rent-seeking behavior. Unless, of course, that something is another cryptocurrency. Those in the Ethereum tribe will ask the question, how could Bitcoin be the winner of DeFi if all the applications are built through Ethereum? Any tribe-like social circle is likely to miss important nuance in their zeal to support their tribe over the other. Ultimately, Bitcoin and Ethereum both play vital roles in the current cryptocurrency ecosystem as it currently stands.

My conclusion is that Bitcoin, as blockchain-based monetary technology, constitutes the fundamental layer of the cryptocurrency ecosystem because it enables the transfer of value in a nonmanipulatable manner. It has a stated use case and stable demand as the only hard money in existence. Ethereum is blockchain-based application technology currently challenging the traditional financial infrastructure. Some will claim that it has the potential to surpass Bitcoin in market capitalization as its applications continue extending outside of finance. Though up for debate, Ethereum plays a role in the portfolio as a slightly more speculative bet on the proliferation of blockchain-based, decentralized applications (DApps). The next chapter will examine ways to incorporate Ethereum and Altcoins into a portfolio while expanding upon the risk/return profile of all digital assets. For most investors, wading into the cryptocurrency ecosystem begins and ends at Bitcoin. For those who want broad exposure to multiple digital assets, one can incorporate Ethereum or invest in a basket of assets on a market capitalization basis unless he or she is willing to conduct the in-depth research required to pick winners and losers. Digital assets such as Ethereum have a proven track record of outperforming Bitcoin for multiple stretches of time, but also contain more downside volatility and are a less proven, less mature market. Including Ethereum is one method of potentially generating additional alpha, but naturally involves more risk.

What Is Ethereum?

Vitalik Buterin published the Ethereum whitepaper in 2013, and the protocol launched in 2015. At its core, Ethereum is a "protocol for building decentralized applications."[3] While Bitcoin has a narrowly focused use case of storing and transferring ownership of coins on a decentralized ledger, Ethereum is the foundational layer by which anyone can program their own smart contracts. It represents the difference between simple and complex commerce, though it has nonfinancial applications such as governance, organizational management, and supply chain management. As mentioned in the previous chapter, a smart contract is essentially an IF, THEN statement. The contract is immutable and no central authority can tamper with the contract or access the funds locked in the contract as it exists on the blockchain. The contract automatically executes to release the funds or facilitate the agreement once the initial conditions are met. Developers can build entire subecosystems, such as decentralized exchanges, on this idea alone.

Ethereum has three primary applications as outlined in its whitepaper: financial, semifinancial, and nonfinancial. Financial applications involve financial derivatives such as stablecoins, decentralized lending, or subtokens that represent other assets. A stablecoin is an asset-backed, or data-feed contract that pegs the price of the coin to the price of another currency or asset. One can also represent ownership of real assets such as art or fractions of real estate through tokenization on the Ethereum network. Semifinancial applications involve money and a nonfinancial aspect. It usually takes the form of an automatically regulated agreement to release funds. For example, insurance companies can automatically process claims once a condition is met or a postal delivery service can automatically release funds once a good is delivered or returned. Lastly, Ethereum has nonfinancial applications such as decentralized file storage platforms or Decentralized Autonomous Organizations (DAOs). In a DAO, the legal framework of a company or community is set in code without the need for a hierarchy or legal team, such that decisions regarding membership, salary, and organizational direction can be made automatically using a majority of votes. Ethereum is similar to a decentralized app store on one's phone or computer. Anyone can build an app on the network, though most projects will fail. Much of the chapter will focus on Ethereum's diverse use cases because it helps readers better understand the asset.

Firstly, Ethereum enabled the Initial Coin Offering (ICO) boom of 2017. In the old economic model, a programmer or entrepreneur with a capital-intensive business idea needed the backing of one or more investors to gain access to the capital required to launch. With the advent of Kickstarter in 2009, potential entrepreneurs could crowdsource their project funds. If the project met its fundraising goal by the deadline, the entrepreneur received the funds and the investors gained partial ownership. If the project did not reach its goal, the investors' funds did not get released. Ethereum automates this process through smart contracts. Coupled with a lack of regulation and a general mania surrounding cryptocurrencies during the 2016 market cycle, some nefarious actors saw this as an opportunity to take advantage of unwitting investors looking to "get rich quick" from the next Bitcoin or Ethereum. One estimate places the amount of capital raised through ICOs in 2017 at $4.9 billion. Excluding 11 projects that returned over 1,000 percent to investors, the median return of the ICO boom was −87 percent.[4]

Even though the craze wreaked of fraud and mismanagement, the concept behind ICOs is still rather revolutionary. Companies such as Kickstarter eliminated the requirement for banks, venture capital, or for an entrepreneur to be geographically located near a financial hub such as New York City, Silicon Valley, or London. Ethereum took this one step further by eliminating the need for centralized companies such as Kickstarter to manage the funding process. Ethereum itself was released via coin offering, raising $18.3 million in Bitcoin in the first month of its launch. The offering went on to pay developer salaries, fund future projects, pay bounties for programmers that can identify and fix bugs, and pay miners. Many projects launched through ICOs were extremely successful, though the unregulated, "wild west" nature of the mania led to investor abuse. This will diminish over time with increased regulation and increased investor knowledge. Ethereum's role in disintermediating centralized authority from the fundraising process serves as one example of DeFi. It also disintermediates banks through collateralized lending, asset tokenization, and U.S. dollar stablecoins.

Readers should understand the difference between centralized and decentralized crypto-lending. BlockFi, SALT lending, Celcius, Gemini, and Coinbase lending programs act no differently than banks. Usually with a 50 percent loan-to-value ratio, no credit check is required. One can take a $25,000 loan by locking up $50,000 worth of Bitcoin as collateral. On a lending protocol such as Aave, Maker, or Compound, smart contracts automate the lending process. One can connect a wallet to the protocol website and take out a loan. However, as opposed to an exchange depositing the funds directly into your bank account, DeFi protocols use dollar stablecoins such as DAI, U.S. Dollar Coin (USDC), or the coin native to that blockchain to deposit funds. In addition to decentralized lending protocols, entire decentralized exchanges (DEx) such as dYdX or Uniswap exist that offer margin trading and greater token selection because they include all Ethereum-based ERC-20 tokens, not just the tokens that centralized exchanges decide to list. Currently, most users will not feel the need to use blockchain technology in every aspect of their financial life. However, with Ethereum-enabled DeFi, anyone can use a protocol to take loans and trade on margin in a trustless ecosystem.

A wide variety of dollar stablecoins exist, but they all serve the same purpose. They are digital dollars that can be used on any DeFi platform. Examples include Tether, USDC, DAI, and exchange tokens such as Binance USD. Why would anyone prefer digital dollar stablecoins over sending dollars through a bank? First, one can send any amount of dollar stablecoins on a DeFI platform or exchange instantaneously and with less fees than wire transfers. Individuals can also hold a zero-volatility asset in their wallet if they want the optionality. Stablecoins also provide a digital rail for anyone to own a dollar-pegged asset outside of a country's financial system. For hyperinflating currencies such as the Venezuelan bolivar or Zimbabwean dollar, the U.S. dollar is a superior store of value. Using DeFi, anyone with exchange access can peg their currency to the dollar to avoid inflationist national policies or capital controls. A third use-case for dollar stablecoins involves remittance payments. Sending dollars through an international money transfer service to one's home country will incur time and fees as high as nine percent. Sending dollar stablecoins to a digital wallet is instant and has a low, flat fee. Ethereum enables the creation of these through digital dollar pegs.

The final financial use case this chapter will examine is the tokenization of real assets, using the real estate example. Companies such as Meridio.co allow for real estate tokenization and fractional ownership. Through the Ethereum network, a commercial property owner can liquidate a portion of his or her property to fund other projects or raise capital. They do this by dividing the property into tokens that represent a certain square footage. Investors who do not have the capital to invest in large real estate projects, but have the desire to do so, can still get exposure by owning fractional shares. Smart contracts automatically distribute the cash flows from the property to all investors. Tokenizing property provides liquidity to the asset owner and exposure to the small investor in an open market. Fundraising without a venture capital firm, purchasing assets without an online broker, exchanging currency for dollars without a currency exchange, and investing in commercial real estate without a bank all represent the power of DeFi.

Ethereum in the Real World

At 2016's Devcon2 Ethereum Conference in Shanghai, China, developers from Etherisc introduced and live-tested a decentralized flight insurance protocol. Customers would pay the application a premium and input flight details. The application would monitor the flight based on the information given, and if canceled or delayed, the smart contract would automatically execute to pay the insured traveler. Of 31 accepted policy applications, 6 experienced flight delays and received their insurance payout. In fact, an insurance payout through the protocol usually reached the traveler before official notification from the airline. The DApp underwent several updates to address critical bugs, including one that allowed insurers to input flights that had already occurred. Despite its initial bugginess, Etherisc had reached a milestone in applying smart contracts to insurance claims. Those in the audience had witnessed a self-executing insurance protocol in real time.

Since then, institutional insurers have demonstrated immense interest self-executing insurance claims. A report by Accenture indicated that the market for blockchain-based insurance will grow at a compound annual rate of 84.9 percent until 2023.[5] Using smart contracts cuts down the need for human resources representatives to process claims and the likelihood of fraud. The cost-savings for insurance companies will be enormous, though it also demonstrates the disrupting effects of technology on jobs. U.S. insurance giant MetLife announced in 2019 that it would introduce a protocol on the Ethereum blockchain to streamline its claims process. Ethereum's applications are only beginning to witness the entrenchment necessary to reach critical mass.

Smart contracts also disrupt supply chain management and identity systems. At its core, the blockchain records exchanges of value between two parties in a secure, verifiable manner. In supply chains, goods and parts exchange hands multiple times in the process that eventually leads to final delivery of a finished product. Through the Ethereum network, one can automatically track the custody of a good, determine the origin of parts, execute payment once the good is received, and maintain a transparent record throughout. Amazon Web Services patented Amazon Managed Blockchain in May 2020, using the Ethereum and Hyperledger Fabric blockchains. The Track and Trace service updates a shared ledger at every stop on the supply chain from supplier to consumer. Using Ethereum for supply chain management prevents fraud and provides full transparency. Twenty-five percent of Ethereum nodes in the world run on Amazon Web Services, and companies such as Nestle, BMW, and Sony Music manage their supply chains through the Ethereum network.[6]

In terms of identity verification, both Bitcoin and Ethereum can cut down on identity theft through cryptographic verification involving public and private keys. Today, governments provide proof of identity through social security cards, passports, driver's licenses, and the like. Bad actors who get a hold of one's personally identifiable information can easily steal someone's identity. They can also create fraudulent government-issued identification cards. These government-issued cards and numbers make a claim that the person is who they say they are, and the only verification, if any, involves photo identification. On any blockchain network, an institution that needs to validate someone's identity can scan that individual's public key. The public key is then signed by the individual's private key to confirm identity. As opposed to physical cards, anyone can have a digital ID on their smart device and sign with their private key to confirm. Cryptographic private keys held behind a firewall of facial recognition and passwords provides more security than a physical social security card or driver's license that can easily be stolen or misplaced. In 2019, Microsoft launched its own decentralized identity tool built on top of the Bitcoin blockchain. Ethereum-based companies such as uPort and ConsenSys provide similar services.

Unlike Bitcoin that had its clearly stated use case at inception, Ethereum opened with the broad-based financial, semifinancial, and non-financial use cases. Since then, the ecosystem has taken a life of its own to power the DeFi movement and has begun migrating to solving real-world problems such as insurance claims and supply chain management. Purchasing Ethereum tokens is akin to owning a share of the protocol and betting on DApps continuing to take market share from traditionally centralized industries. Ethereum mostly challenges the financial industry. Just as Bitcoin challenges government-issued money, Ethereum challenges much of the system that custodies and lends that money.

Bitcoin Versus Ethereum

As the second blue-chip cryptocurrency, Ethereum has both advantages and disadvantages when compared to Bitcoin. Before contrasting the two, I would like to address the idea of their mutual exclusivity. Bitcoin and Ethereum tribalism would have the average investor believe that only one will survive. This tribalism manifests itself in social media, the echo chambers of confirmation bias that only amplify one's sense of tribalism. Seeing as the two coins serve different purposes, I do not see them as challengers to one another. Bitcoin is money. Ethereum is not. Additionally, DeFi projects amplify the decentralization process that Bitcoin began. As decentralized money, Bitcoin segregated governments and banks from the value transaction process. However, adding centralized exchanges as the gatekeepers of Bitcoin, despite their support toward the asset or one's ability to take his or her coins offline, substitutes one form of centralization for another.

The proliferation of decentralized exchanges such as Uniswap, built on the Ethereum protocol, take decentralization one step further by relying on liquidity pools instead of centralized market makers. By using Uniswap, the user must trust the code. Small bugs in code can be fixed, though users must trust that no catastrophic bug exists for hackers to exploit. By using Coinbase or a similar exchange, the user must trust the centralized server and company. Most investors interested in gaining price exposure to cryptocurrencies, seeing as they trust their online bank or online broker to hold their stocks, bonds, and currencies, will have no issue with this. However, a truly bankless, decentralized future will need to see a merge between hard money and smart contracts. Though decentralized exchanges currently only support ERC-20 tokens, several projects exist to create interoperability between blockchains. Bitcoin trading on a decentralized, Ethereum-based platform is inevitable. The concept of wrapped Bitcoin, the 1:1 backed ERC-20 token that currently trades on Ethereum platforms, is only a temporary solution.

In the bigger picture, both Bitcoin and Ethereum are changing money and finance as part of the same ecosystem. If traditional finance involves fiat dollars and traditional banks as the middlemen between value transactions, the parallel blockchain financial system involves hard money in Bitcoin and decentralized programs that reduce reliance on banks. Just as the telephone democratized communication and the Internet democratized access to information, blockchain is democratizing money and finance. Owning Bitcoin, the best-performing asset for the last decade, is the best way to capitalize on this trend and have a stake in the new ecosystem. Owning Ethereum is the second-best investment in this trend, though Ethereum is more volatile and constitutes a more risky investment for reasons that I will address later in this section.

Ethereum is disrupting the world of finance and its price relies on network effects similar to Bitcoin. The main difference between Bitcoin and Ethereum involve their use cases as hard money and blockchain application respectively. However, they contain other differences that potential investors should make themselves aware of. These include a more centralized team of developers, the proof-of-stake mechanism, and undefined scarcity. Active developers and value dilution do not exist in the Bitcoin network and add a component of risk. The second risk is the existential risk of Bitcoin-based smart contracts that programming language does not yet support but one day will. Will the future of DeFi involve inter-blockchain operability protocols that allow Bitcoin to trade on Ethereum networks? Or will it involve a Bitcoin-based smart contracts layer that makes Ethereum obsolete? The rest of this section addresses these differences and risks in order.

The 2016 DAO hack demonstrated both a pro and a con of the Ethereum protocol—the developers could quickly band together to change the protocol if necessary. As previously mentioned, a DAO is a Decentralized Autonomous Organization where a group develops smart contracts to run an organization and conducts an ICO to where number of coins represent voting rights. The DAO, one particular organization launched in April 2016, was a decentralized venture capital organization. Anyone could propose a project and the DAO would vote on whether or not to fund, how much, and even vote on specifics of their ventures. Successful ventures had profits returned to the DAO and its members in

Ethereum. In June 2016, a hacker exposed a bug to successfully drain $70 million, or 3.6 million Ethereum tokens (ETH), from the organization. The price of ETH dropped from $20 to $13, as the DAO contained roughly 15 percent of all ETH.[7]

Days after the attack, Vitalik Buterin and the Ethereum Foundation issued a critical update, saying they had found a solution to the DAO hack. The developers created a soft fork that invalidated any transactions that derived from the DAO or the hacker's "child DAO" through which he or she deposited the funds. Essentially, this fork froze the hacker's assets. The soft fork failed, and hackers continued exploiting the catastrophic bug in the DAO structure to drain its assets. At that point, the core developers of the Ethereum Foundation went one step further in creating a hard fork to return the stolen funds to the DAO, with about 85 percent approval from Reddit polls. This hard fork split the network into Ethereum Classic and Ethereum—with Ethereum Classic being the pre-DAO hack network. Slowly and with controversy, users switched to the network that invalidated the hack. Only about 10 percent of users remained on the classic network.

The issue was not Ethereum itself, but a flaw in the DAO that owned a large percentage of ETH. Imagine if in the 2019 Binance hack, a group of developers banded together to return the funds and freeze the hacker's assets. To some, this fluidity constitutes an advantage of the Ethereum network. To others, it demonstrates troubling centralization that runs counter to the spirit of DeFi projects. It also creates a "too big to fail" moral hazard. When a smaller developer writes a bad contract and loses his or her ETH, the foundation will certainly not go through such efforts to save that organization. Do I personally believe that the Ethereum foundation will undermine the network for their monetary advantage? Of course not. However, investors should know that the Bitcoin governance process involves supermajorities and multiple checks and balances for soft forks alone. The Ethereum governance process is much more centralized as demonstrated by the DAO hack.

In another demonstration of Ethereum's trade-off between centralization and fluidity, updates to the network in Ethereum 2.0 are being rolled out in 2021 and set to complete in 2023. Ethereum 2.0 is not a hard fork and requires no change from current token holders. It provides three major upgrades to the network in an attempt to make it more scalable and secure: the beacon chain, shard chains, and docking. Ethereum 2.0 transitions from proof-of-work to proof-of-stake and reduces the hardware requirement to run a full node on the network. As mentioned in previous chapters, proof-of-stake attributes mining power in direct proportion to the number of coins held, not by computational power and energy. This makes the mining process much less energy intensive and reduces the possibility of a 51 percent attack because one needs to own 51 percent of all ETH, not mining power, to attack the network. The introduction of Ethereum 2.0 reinforces the idea that investors should think of Bitcoin as more of a finished product compared to Ethereum's centrally driven fluidity.

Though Ethereum supporters will claim that proof-of-stake is superior because it is less energy intensive, this energy efficiency does not come without cost. As previously mentioned, proof-of-stake makes it easier for those with large ETH balances to acquire more ETH. Unlike proof of work, there are no forced sellers throughout the mining process. Large ETH holders will inevitably acquire greater voting rights and influence on the future of the protocol. I believe proof-of-stake will inevitably lead to greater centralization. This does not necessarily make Ethereum uninvestable. However, for those who see blockchain technology a wrecking ball to hierarchical structures in money and finance, proof-of-work is a step in the wrong direction. Ethereum 2.0 trades environmental palatability for centralization. For some, this constitutes a necessary tradeoff.

Another major difference between the two networks, and what oftentimes becomes an insurmountable roadblock for Bitcoiners, is Ethereum's undefined scarcity mentioned earlier. The long-term inflation rate of Ethereum trends toward zero, but it does not have Bitcoin's supply cap. Once the transition to proof-of-stake is complete, Ethereum will have an inflation rate between 0 and 5 percent according to its whitepaper.[8] In essence, Ethereum will have an inflation rate similar to gold's as a relatively scarce, but not absolutely scarce asset. Developers created this low inflation rate of coins in order to account for an overconcentration of wealth, lost coins, and flexibility in expanding the coin base. The irony being that wealthy ETH holders have greater staking power to begin with. To hard money enthusiasts, Ethereum developers have the power to dilute shareholder value through coin issuance, making it automatically less valuable than Bitcoin. I would argue that as money, Ethereum does not beat Bitcoin. However, one does not understand Ethereum if they are only examining its monetary qualities.

Ethereum has one major existential threat that blockchain enthusiasts will one day vote on with their wallets. Programmers are currently racing to create a programming language that allows for smart contracts on the Bitcoin network. One programming language called Sapio is built around the CHECKTEMPLATEVERIFY (CTV) code. The Bitcoin network would have to undergo a soft fork to allow for smart contract compatibility through CTV or another method. When asked about Sapio's potential adoption via soft fork in a 2020 interview, Bitcoin contributor and Sapio creator Jeremy Rubin stated, "There are a reasonable amount of people who say it's three years from now—at least."[9] Minsk is another programming language aimed at allowing smart contracts on the Bitcoin network. The trialing process will be extensive for both of these projects even as they reach completion.

Ethereum is also undergoing a process to allow for interoperability between blockchains. Currently, the Ethereum and Bitcoin blockchains run disparate to each other. As previously mentioned, one cannot purchase Bitcoin directly on an Ethereum wallet or DApp, but must purchase wrapped Bitcoin (wBTC), an ERC-20 token backed by Bitcoin. Other cryptocurrencies such as Litecoin and Filecoin also do not operate on Ethereum networks unless wrapped to allow for ERC-20 compatibility. In the real world, that means a supply chain manager using a public blockchain cannot accept Bitcoin as payment, only Ethereum or ERC-20 stablecoins. However, projects such as Cosmos, Chainlink, Polkadot, and Hybrix all aim at creating a network of blockchains that do not operate in a siloed manner. These projects are already launched and will likely allow for interoperability before we witness Bitcoin smart contracts.

Will Bitcoin smart contracts erase the need for Ethereum altogether? Or will using Bitcoin on the Ethereum network be the way forward in DeFi? Though no one can know the definite answer, I believe using a lens of network effects gives us an idea of the most likely scenario. Currently, most of the DeFi ecosystem exists on the Ethereum network. Uniswap reached the milestone of $100 billion cumulative transactions in early 2021. I suspect that number will be much higher by the suggested timeline of 2023 for the rollout of Bitcoin smart contracts, especially if one of the many current projects succeed to allow for greater token interoperability and selection. Will everyone on Uniswap move over to a new, Bitcoin-based decentralized exchange? While Bitcoin purists may, I believe the average user will not. The average user does not care for the mechanics underlying their operating system. They want to know if the exchange is decentralized, operates smoothly, securely, and if it offers the tokens they want to invest in.

Several examples exist to demonstrate how network effects and entrenchment will likely mean that Ethereum applications remain in place despite Bitcoin smart contracts. One example includes the Bitcoin versus Bitcoin Cash debate. As opposed to jumping to a different network altogether, Bitcoin developers upgraded the dominant coin through the lightning network. In terms of smart contracts, Ethereum is the dominant coin. I equate this to interoperability DeFi projects attempting to close the siloes between coins as opposed to the entire space moving to Bitcoin once the technology allows it. Many used the argument of entrenched carmakers introducing electric vehicles as a reason why Tesla will fail, a company that never had a full year of profitability until 2020. Porsche, BMW, and Mercedes all offer luxury electric vehicle alternatives, yet Tesla still has 18 percent of the global electric vehicle market share, with the second largest being Volkswagen at 6 percent.[10] Tesla did not collapse as entrenched carmakers rolled out electric vehicles similar to Zoom not collapsing when Google made its Google Meet feature free in 2020. I do not believe Ethereum will collapse with the introduction of Bitcoin-enabled smart contracts. It certainly has consequences, such as undoing the need for centralization in Bitcoin-based loans, though I do not believe DeFi will shift to Bitcoin-only platforms. Despite this, investors should understand the risk that this technology could take significant market share from certain Ethereum's DApps. Similar to how Bitcoin had a scalability issue that it needed to solve in 2016, Ethereum has an interoperability issue that it must overcome for mass adoption.

On Altcoins

All "alternative coins" to Bitcoin and Ethereum fall under the umbrella of Altcoins, although some will claim that the title goes to any blockchain-based digital asset that is not Bitcoin. I categorize Altcoins into four types—cryptocurrencies, security tokens, utility tokens, and DeFi protocols. Though many in the blockchain community will disagree with my characterizations seeing as DeFi protocols can be also be security and utility tokens, I believe this narrower characterization more neatly describes the ecosystem.

The first type of Altcoins are cryptocurrencies, or Bitcoin alternatives whose purpose is to make payments and store value in a secure, decentralized manner. Examples include Bitcoin Cash, Litecoin, Monero, and Zcash. Some currencies emphasize network speed for greater use in microtransactions, improving on the prelightning network limitations of Bitcoin. Others have enhanced privacy features such as Monero's stealth addresses and Zcash's zero knowledge-proof transactions that make them less trackable than Bitcoin's use of public addresses. Personally, any token that advertises itself as a Bitcoin alternative is not worth the investment. Bitcoin is by far the dominant monetary network that accomplishes the primary functions of money as a medium of exchange and store of value. Institutions are not racing to provide Litecoin or Zcash services. All other coins that aim to take market share from Bitcoin will either fade into irrelevance as they fail to gain the same network effects or remain relegated into niche markets—such as illicit or private transactions that would warrant a more private monetary network.

The second type of Altcoins are security tokens. I include stablecoins under this umbrella. Security tokens are an interesting use case of blockchain technology whereby an asset becomes tokenized and ownership becomes preserved on the blockchain ledger. Though algorithmic stablecoins exist that expand and contract supply in order to maintain a certain peg, most stablecoins serve as securitized tokens of a different asset. That asset can be U.S. dollars in the case of the USDC token or exchange based stablecoins. The collateralized asset can also be commodities such as the Digix Gold token on the Ethereum network, or specific real estate markets such as the New York City Real Estate Coin or the SwissRealCoin. They can also be collateralized by other Digital Assets, such as the DAI token that is overcollaterized by ETH to maintain its dollar peg and cushion against negative volatility. Investable protocols such as Synthetix and Universal Market Access (UMA) create synthetic financial instruments to track the price of other investments using their tokens as collateral. Though they have different system designs, these are both derivative protocols. Synthetix offers short Ethereum and short Bitcoin tokens, short fiat currency tokens, or tokens such as iDEFI that inversely tracks a basket of DeFi protocols. Derivatives tokens, similar to derivatives-based ETFs, is a largely untapped market that will provide greater asset selection to investors on a decentralized exchange. UMA is set to launch an S&P 500 index token, for example. In the future, I believe all financial securities will also trade in tokenized form on decentralized exchanges. Will everyone migrate to decentralized exchanges and purchase S&P 500 tokens as opposed to the index on their brokerage account? Unlikely. However, in an attempt to avoid trade commissions, brokerage fees, mutual fund management fees, broker risk, and trade on a 24-hour basis, there will undoubtedly be a market for decentralized trading. Financial securities tokenization is an exciting aspect of blockchain technology still in its early stages.

The next type of Altcoin is the utility token. Utility tokens provide a user with a product or service, although the value of the token may increase as more users interact with a limited supply of token issuances. Tradable tokens exist to provide file storage renting, computing power renting, identity verification, digital advertising solutions, and more. Some utility tokens power a rental agreement between users while others power an entire ecosystem. Filecoin, Siacoin, and Storj are examples of peer-to-peer file storage protocols. In Filecoin (FIL), for example, miners are rewarded with coins for providing excess disc space for storage. Users can pay any miner with FIL to store their files at rates that are usually more competitive than cloud-based storage systems. The Golem Network (GNT) works in a similar manner replacing file storage capacity with excess computing power. Individual computers and large data centers alike can earn GNT for renting out their Central Processing Unit (CPU) power. In terms of ecosystem-based tokens, Civic is an identity verification ecosystem that does not rely on centralized databases to store usernames and passwords. Participants in the ecosystem get rewarded with Civic coins. The Basic Attention Token (BAT) is the native token of the Brave browser that transforms digital marketing by paying web surfers in BAT for their attention placed to advertisements. Utility tokens power a service. While the token price may appreciate depending on the popularity of the protocol, they are not collateralized securities or intended currencies outside of their ecosystem.

The last type of Altcoins, though some would claim that they fall under security or utility token depending on their use case, is the DeFi protocol. These include decentralized lending protocols such as Compound and Aave and decentralized exchange protocols such as the Uniswap token used in governance or the Bancor Network Token used as a default currency for that network. They also include tokens specific to smart contract operability such as oracle networks, which exist as third-party tokens that feed smart contracts with the external data they require. Chainlink, Augur, which specializes in prediction markets, and the Band Protocol are examples of oracle tokens that provide necessary information to smart contracts. Cosmos and THORChain are examples of protocols tackling the previously mentioned blockchain interoperability issue.

Bitcoin and Ethereum have monopolies in the digital currency and smart contracts spaces respectively. One shortfall of investing in the Altcoin space involves the nuance between protocols competing for limited market share. For example, I believe blockchain interoperability and derivatives tokens constitute two promising DeFi trends with market oligopolies. Will the oligopoly remain so? Will a current token become the dominant network in that field? Will a new token achieve the desired end-state in a manner that makes the current protocols obsolete? Unlike the blue-chip digital assets, these technologies are new and early in their adoption curves. They have the potential to become the backbones of a tokenized digital asset market that rivals traditional stock markets. They also have the potential to go to zero. An in-depth study of the over 5,000 Altcoins that exist will be a largely fruitless endeavor, especially when there is so much alpha generated in the Bitcoin and Ethereum spaces already. The subsequent chapter will examine what role, if any, Altcoins can play in a portfolio.

Aside from providing definitions, examples, and personal commentary on Ethereum and Altcoins, I hope this chapter cleared up the misconceptions many investors have. Though the precious metals analogy makes sense for Bitcoin, Ethereum and Altcoins are not the silver and platinum to Bitcoin's digital gold. Additionally, the term *cryptocurrency* is a misnomer. Currencies have historically had three functions: that of a medium of exchange, store of value, and unit of account. Most digital assets were not created with these functions in mind. Each digital asset serves a unique purpose, hence why the more nebulous term *digital asset* fits better than cryptocurrency. Collateralized tokens have more in common with securities than currencies. Utility tokens may be the native currency of their respective networks, but exist within niche markets such as file storage and online advertising. Smart contracts, exchange governance tokens, and oracle protocols all share the use case of powering DeFi, having nothing to do with daily purchases that one would equate with a currency. Treating all these tokens as alternative currencies is a gross misrepresentation.

CHAPTER 8

Digital Assets in Your Portfolio

In July 2020, I wrote an article on Seeking Alpha titled "The Anti-Fragile Portfolio," detailing how permanently low rates and moderate to high inflation will place a premium on scarce assets. While I originally stated that Bitcoin and gold can both fulfill that role, I have since come to the realization that Bitcoin is a much more direct investment for profiting from the end of monetary policy. A motor vehicle and horse and buggy will never drive on the same road. Bitcoin perfects the qualities that made gold attractive in the first place and obsoletes the paper dollar initially created as a receipt for gold. Following is the expanded summary of my conclusion in that article:

> The financial system cannot handle deflation or excess inflation. The pension system cannot afford for stocks to go down and governments cannot afford for yields to rise. The Fed will continue juggling these fragilities and keep the system afloat as a matter of policy... because this system is so fragile, investors should also load up on insurance in the form of gold and Bitcoin.[1]

With the current debt load, persistent deflation will create a shockwave of defaults. Small business not making sufficient profits will forego making payments on leased commercial property, which will make the landlord at risk of not making mortgage payments, will make the bank at risk of being undercapitalized. Quickly inflating the debt away may be akin to pressing the reset button on the national debt, but threatens the hegemony of the dollar and will surely increase social tensions. Underfunded pension systems will not meet their obligations if stocks mean revert, and the consumption-based economy will suffer in tandem.

Paying $522 billion in interest payments on the national debt alone in 2020 with rates at near zero, rising rates will place pressure on fiscal programs already being funded through deficit spending.[2] The Fed will have to print more money and purchase more bonds to keep yields low if inflation threatens to create a Minsky moment in the bond market. Central planners put the U.S. economy in a corner whereby printing is the only thing preventing widespread defaults.

The "Anti-Fragile Portfolio" was not a way to trade around the inefficiencies created by Central Banks, but a portfolio built for the multidecade paradigm shift that will occur as we reach the limits of debt-based easing and begin devaluation-based easing. With rates hovering near zero, the incentive to take out more debt and pull aggregate demand forward does not exist unless rates go negative. Inflating the debt away is the most likely way forward as signaled by central bankers themselves. As the scarcest asset available in a fragile monetary dynamic whose only way forward involves printing money to finance public deficits, the attractiveness of Bitcoin is clear. Add its diminutive market capitalization compared to traditional financial assets and its role as monetary technology that supplants both payment networks and gold, and Bitcoin all of a sudden becomes both a hedge and a high-powered growth asset. It clearly should play a role in every portfolio. Whether that percentage is 1 percent, 5 percent, 15 percent, or all of the portfolio is up to the individual investor's stomach for volatility as digital assets have historically fallen by greater than 80 percent in bear markets and oftentimes correct 30 percent in bull markets.

Yet volatility is not risk. What I hope the previous excerpt from the article demonstrates is the fact that the traditional financial system, due to decades of central planning, has plenty of built-in risk. At this point, the Fed's unwillingness to intervene in financial markets in the speed or scope required will threaten the pension system, the government's ability to spend, and corporation's ability to operate. They need to intervene and that intervention will support Bitcoin more than the bubbles being reflated. I believe all investors should "get off zero" in terms of their Bitcoin investment. I also believe that for most investors, the journey into digital assets begins and ends at Bitcoin. In the past decade, Bitcoin has provided a 200 percent compound annual growth rate compared to the S&P's 12 percent. With such growth rates and Bitcoin continuing to earn credibility among institutions, the concept of reaching for more yield in the crypto ecosystem seems superfluous. But what if, understanding all this, one truly believes in the power of blockchain technology to reorganize the traditional financial infrastructure and the way many businesses operate?

At the end of the day, investments are bets. The investor soaks in all available information, calculates the probabilities of future outcomes, and allocates capital accordingly. The belief that Bitcoin will join the ranks of traditional financial assets and payment networks due to its unique qualities, and the belief that decentralized applications will continue to proliferate and bring value to the Ethereum network, are two mostly mutually exclusive bets with the only relation being the blockchain technology that underlies them. Investing in a basket of cryptocurrencies is taking an asymmetric bet that blockchain-based digital assets will continue to disrupt the current financial system, potentially creating a parallel one or supplanting it altogether. One is also betting that a few specific tokens will be the ones making this change. Before adding other digital assets to a portfolio, investors must first understand the risk involved.

The Digital Asset Risk Curve

A risk curve visually depicts the relationship between risk and reward among investments. On the x-axis is perceived risk and on the y-axis is return. In the financial system risk curve, bonds have less risk and less return than do stocks than do venture capital or private equity. The implicit assumption in any risk curve is that more volatile assets are inherently more risky. Though I believe the digital asset space follows this assumption, I do not agree that it is always necessarily true. Bonds have experienced low volatility over a 40-year bull market that stems from the Fed reaction function of lowering rates in the face of economic weakness. An interventionist Central Bank makes traditional assets less volatile, but compounding debt when the cause of the recession is too much debt creates greater structural risk. With no third-party intervention, the digital asset risk curve includes not only volatility, but also the risk of losing all one's capital altogether. Making the determination of which assets can potentially go to zero involves some subjectivity. For the risk curve, I will include three assets: Bitcoin, Ethereum, and the entire Altcoin space.

In the digital asset risk curve, Bitcoin constitutes the asset with the least risk and reward—a difficult idea to conceptualize given a 200 percent compound annual growth rate since inception. Writing in February 2021, the year-to-date (YTD) return on Bitcoin is 93.3 percent compared to the S&P's 4.0 percent. Of course, every indicator tells me we are in the middle-to-late stages of a bull market. Bitcoin is the most mature market with the most institutional entrenchment. Any risk to this asset involves political risk given that it challenges government's sovereignty over money, though this risk diminishes each passing week with continued corporate entrenchment and the aforementioned applied game theory informing investors that governments will profit more from embracing than fighting it. In terms of volatility as measured by the standard deviation of annualized returns, Bitcoin achieved 65.5 percent compared to Ethereum's 75.15 percent for 2019. For perspective, Tesla's stock had 58.7 percent during that same period.

The YTD return for Ethereum is 167.9 percent. Ethereum's tendency to outperform Bitcoin during stretches of digital asset bull markets is an idea that gets lost in most media outlets seeing as Bitcoin tends to define the space. At six years younger than Bitcoin, Ethereum is a less mature market with a smaller user base and market capitalization, which gives it more volatility than Bitcoin. Additionally, Ethereum has centralization risk, inflation risk, and the silver bullet for many Bitcoiners, existential risk in looming Bitcoin smart contracts that warrant its status as a more risky investment. Given that Ethereum has a larger market capitalization than Bitcoin had at its six-year mark, some investors believe that it may one day surpass Bitcoin. If the Ethereum maximalist dream comes true of a new decentralized financial system supplanting banks, this may well be the case. However, Ethereum had the advantage of Bitcoin having paved the way for the introduction of additional digital assets.

The YTD performance for UMA and Cosmos, two protocols specializing in derivative tokens and blockchain interoperability respectively, are 236 percent and 275 percent. Thus far, these constitute two successful digital asset projects. Both projects have immense risk being less than three years old and with several tokens competing for market share in the same fields. Though annualized volatility in UMA, for example, will be difficult to find given that it was publicly listed on Coinbase in September 2020, statistics show that Altcoins are inherently more volatile than Bitcoin and Ethereum. UMA fell by 35 percent on September 5, 2020, the same month it was listed. All statistics on volatility versus returns in the digital asset ecosystem demonstrate a risk curve that closely resembles the following figure (Figure 8.1). I included traditional financial assets for investors to remember that the risk/return profile of digital assets is leagues away from stocks and bonds. With 8 percent to 200 percent returns between the S&P and Bitcoin since the latter's inception, the gap in the following risk curve is arguably not wide enough.

Some Altcoins may experience a Mt. Gox or DAO hack moment that threatens the protocol's existence. Or another coin can still gain network effects and surpass them given their relative newness and small market capitalization. Altcoins are the furthest point in the risk curve given that most of the 5,000+ coins in existence will fail. Similar to venture capital, I believe the Pareto Principle can inform investors of the potential distribution of returns in this subset. The Pareto Principle is named after Italian economist Vilfredo Pareto. First noticing that 20 percent of the families in Italy owned 80 percent of the property, he began expanding this idea to other aspects of the physical world, concluding that most things follow a power curve as opposed to a normal distribution. The principle states that 80 percent of the consequences derive from 20 percent of the inputs. In work, that means 20 percent of the employees will by themselves complete 80 percent of the work. In markets, it states that 20 percent of one's investments will create 80 percent of the profits. Investors have found ways to take advantage of power curve distributions. For one, large, concentrated bets are both the fastest way to make a fortune when correct and the fastest way to lose a fortune when incorrect.

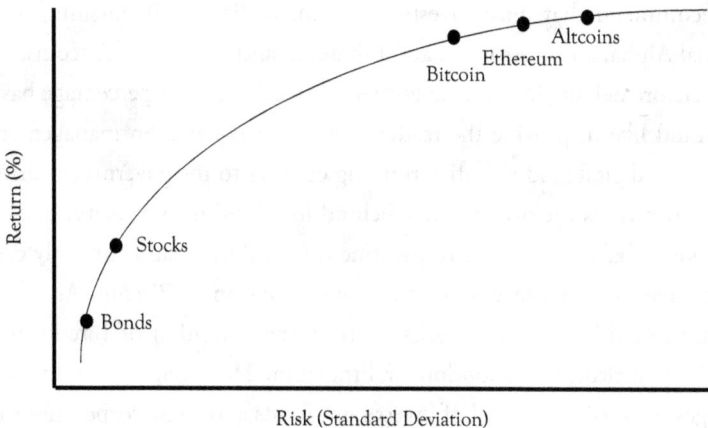

Figure 8.1 Digital asset risk curve

In the highly speculative world of early stage investing such as venture capital or angel investing, returns demonstrate an exaggerated power curve. According to one study, 50 percent of venture capital investments will return less than the capital invested.[3] Six percent of the deals will provide greater than 10× returns and 60 percent of the entire portfolio profit. The rest of the deals fall in the range of 1× to 10× returns. High-performing funds even had more failed investments than mediocre funds in what's aptly described as the Babe Ruth Effect—always swinging for the fences will lead to more strikeouts but inevitably more homeruns. Of course, picking home run investments out of a crowd of potential investments is just as much of an art as it is a statistical science. As a rule of thumb, I believe Altcoin investments follow a similar distribution to venture capital investments. Of 10 Altcoin investments, half will go to zero, 3 will provide average returns, and 2 may be home run investments. For a vast majority of investors without the time to conduct in-depth due diligence on highly speculative Altcoins, I recommend staying away. If one decides to venture that far out into the digital asset risk curve, diversify into a large basket of tokens and expect half of the investments to never turn a profit.

Performance across digital assets highlights certain aspects that exist in every risk curve. During phases of risk-on, such as the middle of a bull market, investors gain the confidence required to wade further out into the risk curve. Given the smaller markets of Ethereum and Altcoins, they tend to outperform for periods of time. During periods of risk-off, such as any bear market, riskier assets fall farther than their less risky counterparts. Because the digital asset space contains enough risk as it is, I recommend that most investors remain in Bitcoin. If pursuing additional Alpha, an investor can add Ethereum and a basket of Altcoins.

Before delving into the investment frameworks on a percentage basis, I would like to provide the reader with some expectation management. Bitcoin's digital gold narrative running counter to the government printing narrative is the driving force behind its adoption as a reserve asset in corporate balance sheets and investment funds. Ethereum currently does not have the same level of institutional adoption as Bitcoin. As a later section of this chapter suggests, institutional adoption of Bitcoin may lead to institutional adoption of Ethereum. However, Ethereum challenges the business model of investment funds and some corporations by providing the same services on a decentralized basis. An investment fund placing capital in Ethereum is similar to Kodak investing in the iPhone that displaced it. I do not see Ethereum's path following the same footsteps as Bitcoin. The financial and corporate old guard will likely not play as significant a role in its price appreciation. An investment in Ethereum and Ethereum-based protocols is a bet on two occurrences: (1) The future of finance is decentralized. (2) The winner of decentralized finance will be Ethereum. Though the current distribution of returns and volatility clearly points to Ethereum as one step further than Bitcoin in the digital asset risk curve, a new public narrative can easily deter this concept, and delving into other digital assets is not guaranteed to generate additional alpha even though the data currently suggests otherwise.

Three Investment Frameworks

That being said, how do we incorporate knowledge of the digital asset risk curve and bullishness on the entire digital asset space into a coherent investment framework? It begins with the investor deciding how much to allocate and through what medium, though I will provide my admittedly biased personal opinion here. For one, the digital asset space is incredibly polarizing. Investors tend to gain a religious-like zeal and go all-in or proverbially bury their heads in the sand and call the space a bubble. The latter is usually an intellectually lazy judgment call that an investor made without any due diligence. Just now gaining institutional traction, a "forward thinking" investment advisor may pitch 1 to 5 percent digital asset allocation of total investable assets as part of a diversified portfolio in a tax-advantaged account to gain upside exposure without risking too much capital. Personally, I believe most advisors are too late and too low; but naturally, if an entrenched financial actor relies on a continuation of the status quo to make their livelihood, they will be incredibly risk averse and tend to follow the herd.

I also believe that most people severely underestimate the role that blockchain-based digital assets will play in the future financial system. Even though 5 percent may be a suitable entry point for most investors who are not accustomed to the volatility, using a brokerage account does not provide the flexibility of a digital wallet in terms of asset selection, the ability to send and receive tokens with other wallets, and the ability to cold store Bitcoin. One gains price exposure, not a stake in a decentralized future or a sense of ownership in the underlying. In practical terms, the investor is also likely to pay too high a premium through traditional brokerage options that may not even exist in half a century. Understanding the practical difference between custody and price exposure, Goldman Sachs, Fidelity, and Deutsche Bank are all entering the digital asset space through custody solutions, not solely trading in open markets. For the sake of argument, let's assume this investor chooses to open a digital wallet with 5 percent of his or her liquid capital.

The first framework involves the investor remaining in the most mature market of the risk curve. The entire percentage goes to Bitcoin and the investor will have plenty of upside exposure with only one asset to monitor. He or she can take a passive role and rebalance with other investments annually, or a more active role and de-risk according to the valuation metrics presented in Chapter 4. The second framework involves adding Ethereum to the Bitcoin investment on a market capitalization basis. Here, the investor is adding a component of risk for potential reward. The market capitalization of Ethereum is roughly one-fifth of Bitcoin's. That provides a 5:1 ratio, or roughly 83 percent Bitcoin to 17 percent Ethereum. The final framework involves adding a basket of very early-stage Altcoin projects, also on a market capitalization basis. After removing the top 10 digital assets from the entire crypto market capitalization, the entire Altcoin space at the time of this writing is $222 billion, roughly equivalent to the size of Ethereum. Using a 5:1:1 ratio, we arrive at 71 percent Bitcoin, 14 percent Ethereum, and 14 percent a basket of 5 to 10 Altcoins. Of course, this option requires a higher level of due diligence and the expectation that half of the Altcoins will not yield the investor anything. It also risks that investors willingly enter the hamster wheel of constantly chasing yield in the Altcoin space when, even though the risk curve seems clear at the moment, Bitcoin indexation may be the winning strategy in the end. Simply buying and holding Bitcoin has outperformed every complex investment fund strategy to date.

Valuing Digital Assets

Digital assets are unique in that the increasing value of the network due to Metcalfe's Law is directly reflected in price. This contrasts to regular networks such as Facebook or Google where the network and user base are created first, then monetized through ad revenue or some other means. Raoul Pal, founder of Real Vision Group and Macro Insiders, uncovered a fascinating relationship between Bitcoin and Ethereum in a January 2021 article titled "The Inconvenient Truth About Cryptocurrencies."[4] The truth is that Ethereum has the exact same distribution of price to active users as did Bitcoin six years into its existence. Starting at one million active addresses, the point that Pal believes digital assets achieve critical mass, the price of Ethereum from 2016 to 2021 matches almost exactly with Bitcoin from 2013 to 2018 in both price and number of users. Altcoins follow the same distribution as well. Digital asset networks have a shockingly simple value proposition—more users on the network lead to a higher token price in a very predictable manner.

The conclusion here is that no other metric matters besides the adoption rate. A growing user base leads to exponential price action due to Metcalfe's Law. If the value is in the user base, the only winning strategies include investing in established tokens that have already achieved critical mass and are expected to steadily increase, or identifying early-stage tokens that offer a service with a high likelihood of achieving critical mass. Therefore, investing in digital asset protocols is more akin to investing in private companies than publicly listed equities, as owning a scarce number of tokens in that protocol equates to owning a piece of the network. Though protocols will differ in their specifics, it pays to find a growing network and to find it early.

There are also some caveats to Pal's point that should be addressed. For one, with institutional adoption, the relationship between number of active users and token price will become even more exponential because institutional capital is multitudes deeper than the individual retail investor. Additionally, if network effects is the driving force behind adoption, is the SF model just smoke and mirrors? The answer is a resounding no. Cyclical supply shocks undoubtedly affect price when assuming steady demand. As price action begets public attention, begets more users, begets further price action, we enter a reflexive loop that drives the Bitcoin price to nosebleed territory. The price action of Ethereum and Altcoins, driven by additional users, move according to Bitcoin's SF model as the following chart demonstrates (Figure 8.2). Ethereum and Chainlink have no

COINMETRICS

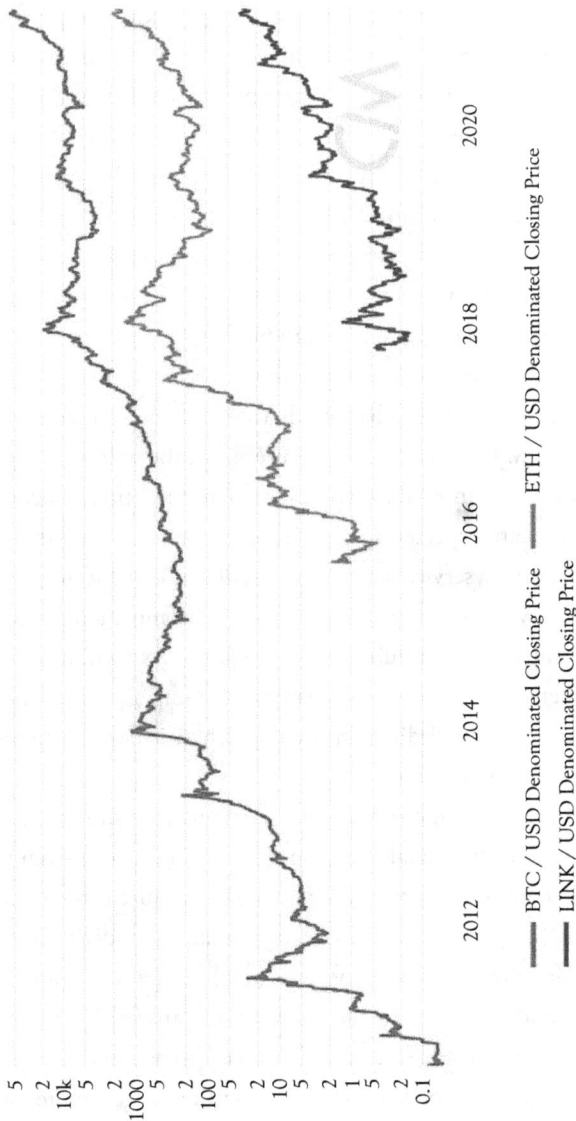

BTC / USD Denominated Closing Price ——— ETH / USD Denominated Closing Price
LINK / USD Denominated Closing Price

Figure 8.2 Digital assets following BTC/USD

fundamental supply shocks or similar aspects that would intrinsically lead to such behavior. The price action results from what Santiago Velez of Block Digital Corporation labels the Bitcoin liquidity waterfall.

The Bitcoin Liquidity Waterfall

The theory proposed by Velez is part of his larger framework aligning with Pal's that network effects are the true force behind price action in digital assets. It states that Bitcoin acts as a "gateway drug" for investors to begin examining and investing in other digital assets. For most, Bitcoin is the digital asset with the highest value proposition—the only hard money that exists in a world of high-powered money printing. This value proposition outweighs the switching costs from fiat to Bitcoin. Switching costs include the learning curve with regard to digital assets, creating a digital wallet, and initial concerns that the investor might lose a majority of his or her capital. The value proposition must also outweigh that of competitors, lest Bitcoin become the Myspace to another asset's Facebook. As mentioned in previous chapters, I find this incredibly unlikely given Bitcoin's current network effects and institutional adoption rate.

Less established digital assets do not have the value proposition to justify the high switching costs from fiat to their token. Most investors will not move from dollars to Chainlink, for example. However, once a Bitcoin wallet is established, the switching costs between digital assets is incredibly low. From a time and fees perspective, it is simpler to switch from Bitcoin to Ethereum than from Bitcoin to equities in a separate brokerage account. Not only does this make intuitive sense, but the liquidity waterfall deriving from Bitcoin explains why all digital assets follow an SF model even when they have no intrinsic reason for doing so. As the Bitcoin network grows or shrinks, the Ethereum and Altcoin networks follow suit due to the low switching costs. The conclusion is that once investors surmount the initial hurdle of investing in Bitcoin, they tend to stay and explore other assets before going back to fiat. This has important implications for the rest of the digital asset space as institutions are just now adding Bitcoin to their balance sheets or creating trading desks. This theory suggests that institutions will eventually begin exploring Ethereum and Altcoin investments before putting that cash back on their balance sheets. Additionally, knowing that low switching costs effect the user base, investors in tokens other than Bitcoin should keep a watchful eye on regulatory factors that affect switching costs.

For some, the answer of user base, network effects, and a liquidity waterfall from Bitcoin to address the value of Altcoins will not be satisfactory. Similar to early-stage investing, these tokens have no cash flow and high volatility. Therefore, investors should take a similar approach when examining digital assets. The value of every network derives from its user base. The key to understanding the value of FAANG stocks involves understanding scalable network growth and margins for the product or service. A decentralized digital currency or financial protocol will not have margins. Value is decided on the free market through the interaction of limited supply and network adoption.

Conclusion

Since 1960, the U.S. M2 money supply has grown at an average of 7.02 percent. It eclipsed 10 percent following the 2008 Global Financial Crisis and reached an eye-popping 25 percent in 2020 following a full embrace of deficit spending in the wake of the pandemic. U.S. GDP growth has averaged 3.17 percent for the same time period, though began trending lower after 2008 to average 2 percent. Logic would dictate that the historic inflation rate is roughly 4 percent, or the devaluation rate accounting for growth. Yet inflation from 2011 to 2021, as measured by a basket of goods in the Consumer Price Index (CPI), has averaged 1.71 percent. The discrepancy results in the incredibly flawed nature of inflation measuring. If medical costs inflate at a compounding annual rate of 6 percent according to Price Waterhouse Cooper Health Research Institute, and health care accounts for 17.7 percent of GDP, then 1.06 percent of total inflation results from health care alone.[1] CPI would dictate that the other 80.3 percent of the economy inflates at only 0.7 percent. Any consumer knows this is not true.

Do not be fooled by economists saying there is no inflation. Though the prices of certain goods and services may not increase on a demand basis with money remaining in the financial system, a 4 percent historical monetary debasement rate serves as a more accurate measure of true inflation than CPI. Newly created money has no backing and no value. It robs value from the currency already in circulation. In 2020, with M2 growth achieving 25 percent and GDP growth at negative 3.5 percent, the mechanism by which governments spend money by taking value from the savings, wages, and investments of its populace has entered Mach 5. Through debasement, governments collateralize the future productivity of people to spend in the present.

Monetary debasement pushes investors farther and farther out into the risk curve as their safe investments lose value over time. With negative rates in some parts of the world, sovereign debt is perhaps the antithesis of a store of value. At 2 to 3 percent yield, high-grade corporate debt does not hold value at even half of the debasement rate. At 4 percent, junk bonds yield less than the rate at which the companies typically default. With defensive sectors in equities failing to perform as well, only high-growth, low-debt technology stocks and private markets provide even a semblance of yield in our economic system. Nearly the entire public markets space fails as a store of value against monetary debasement. As investors unknowingly migrate to riskier and riskier assets, public markets become more of a casino than a way to own shares of the cash flows and growth of a business. Satoshi was correct in saying that governments will always breach the trust placed in them to maintain a steady monetary base. The second- and third-order effects of that breach reverberates through our social, economic, and political systems.

The unfortunate truth is that it takes a broken economic system for an independent, digital hard money to grow at 200 percent year over year. Bitcoin is a black hole that extracts yield from all of the failing stores of value in public markets. Most notably the bond markets but equities as well. It will continue sucking market capitalization from traditional investments as the only absolutely scarce and absolutely liquid asset in existence. If I could travel to 1980 and invest my money according to the seismic shifts of the time, I would leverage a portfolio of stock, bonds, and real estate as everything inflated in the wake of the Federal Reserve suppressing the cost of capital to combat the business cycle. From 1980 to 2020, anyone who employed this strategy became very rich. The next seismic shift already occurred, and the world is only waking up to it now. Scarce, blockchain-based digital assets is the only investment that outpaces the rate of M2 growth and Fed balance sheet expansion. Bitcoin is the next 40-year bond bull market, only its yield will be much higher.

Gold investors are in the ballpark to value a scarce asset outside of the financial system, but they will underperform as they race their horse and buggy against a motorized vehicle. Equity investors focusing on growth are closer, yet missing the driving force behind price appreciation and they will also underperform. Meanwhile, those searching for yield in fixed income are not even on the right planet. Monetary expansion may allow their investments to tread water, but expecting price appreciation after a 40-year bull market with rates near zero and fiscal stimulus threatening markets with higher CPI prints is a dangerous game indeed.

If there is one truth to be obtained from the half century of compounding economic inefficiencies, it is that you cannot plan an economy. In fact, the economy plans you. Entering a job market with tens of thousands of dollars of student debt and real-estate prices at all-time highs will incur different behavior from entering a job market before inflation had a chance to raise the costs of desirable goods such as education and homes. An economy that provides exorbitant privilege to actors with access to capital will see its intellectual capital flow to those sectors. There will be no shortage of lawyers, bankers, and politicians under the fiat system. The safest avenue to personal success in any fiat system involves inching one's way closer to the easy money spicket. The second safest avenue was not an option until Bitcoin. It involves allocating a certain percentage of net worth to antifragile assets that will outpace debasement and resting assured that your value will not be destroyed. Corporations and governments are waking up to this and placing Bitcoin on their balance sheets.

Most things in economics is a zero-sum game. Take minimum wage, for example. Increasing minimum wage to a certain level is perfectly fine, but expect those additional costs on businesses to be passed on to consumers through higher prices for goods and services or in the labor market through less hiring overall. The decision is neither right nor wrong, only a reallocation of priorities. The same concept applies to manipulating interest rates. Doing so is fine to escape a current recession, but expect the level of debt to increase over what would be considered normal levels and expect that debt burden to have second-order impacts. Compound those inefficiencies for decades and markets stumble from crisis to crisis. Printing money is fine to plug the holes of lost capital in an economy, but expect debasement in wages and savings to create social tensions, and expect greater risk-taking behavior as most investments cannot outpace the debasement rate.

I have heard very intelligent people tell me they do not understand the digital asset space and I hope this book clarifies any doubts or concerns. For Bitcoin evangelists, I hope this book enlightens the risks that exist to the network. Global collaboration to stop Bitcoin adoption, derivatives markets, and geostrategic risks in Chinese mining constitute some of these risks. Personally, I believe the CBDC and Bitcoin route provides an outlet for governments to escape the Fed trap. Targeted fiscal spending provides money to those who need it by skipping banks. As velocity of money dies at bank balance sheets, fiscal programs will reach those most in need, but likely create an increase in CPI as opposed to an increase in the price of risk assets. Additionally, Bitcoin protects from competitive devaluation on a sovereign level better than gold.

I also hope that this book illuminates some of the positive aspects of Ethereum and a subsect Altcoins for Bitcoin evangelists as well. I understand perfectly well that I lost some Bitcoin maximalists with that sentence. If one is not convinced of the potential of smart contracts to disintermediate most financial actors or Altcoin protocols to provide specific services that provide value to the digital asset ecosystem, then at least believe in the statistical relationship between volatility, returns, and liquidity flows among digital assets. Whether one chooses to profit from these relationships is up to them. While Bitcoin is and likely will always be the backbone of my digital asset portfolio, I believe Ethereum has reached critical mass in network effects and will continue to appreciate in price with Bitcoin, perhaps even outpacing it at times. I own some on the asymmetric bet that it will serve as the basis of an alternative financial system.

Occam's razor is a philosophical concept stating that the simplest explanation, or the one with the least variables, is usually the correct one. I have found this concept as a useful guide when explaining the value propositions of Bitcoin, Ethereum, and Altcoins. If citizens had a choice between soft and hard money, I believe they would choose hard money. Why? It allows one to store the value acquired from labor or services for future use. It allows the actor to choose what to do with his or her money. With soft money, compounding inflation forces economic actors into putting that money into the economy to avoid devaluation. It pulls aggregate demand forward. Though a boon for post-Keynesian economists, economies run into issues when all future productivity has been mortgaged to finance spending in the present.

For the first time ever, investors have the choice to allocate some capital in a hard money asset. Remembering Occam's razor, hard money beats soft money by providing the owner freedom of choice. Occam's razor is why I value the stock-to-flow model more than on-chain analytics, though the latter certainly informs my investment decisions. Bitcoin continues appreciating at high rates as high adoption rates meet limited supply. Digital assets constitute the only network where an increased user base is directly reflected in the price per coin. Adoption rates depend on the value proposition, whether it be a hard money network or a block-chain application layer. This framework applies to all digital assets.

I have found that those most resistant to digital assets are those with the most self-preservation bias. These include mainstream economists, fund managers, and public intellectuals with the most to lose from digital asset adoption. Understanding the ecosystem takes due diligence, believing in the future of the ecosystem takes faith that entrenched institutions will continue embracing it, and placing capital in the ecosystem takes courage. This book is one step in the right direction in terms of due diligence and facts to combat a faith-based approach.

Investing is a fascinating intellectual pursuit because one generates a thesis based on the information available and tests it in real time with real capital. A correct thesis is rewarded with additional capital and an incorrect thesis with a reduction of capital. My thesis is that digital assets broadly, and Bitcoin specifically, constitute a generational investment opportunity in the birth of an antifragile asset class that stores value better than any asset that currently exists. Critics will state that its price volatility prevents it from serving as a store of value. I would contend that they have the wrong time horizon, and at 200 percent growth annually against an ever-increasing debasement rate, they seem to argue that it stores value too well. Furthermore, Bitcoin critics have been spectacularly wrong for over a decade. Though time will tell if their fortunes will reverse, I believe the wheels are set in motion to create widespread institutional adoption of Bitcoin in western economies and among nation states. Proliferation of Bitcoin will only lead to greater adoption of Ethereum and other digital assets. I hope this book provided value to each reader in their investment journey. My perspective is one of many and I encourage investors to understand all perspectives before allocating capital.

Notes

Chapter 1

1. Reuters (2020).
2. Daly (2020).
3. Kaylani (2019).
4. Ammous (2018).
5. Gromen et al. (2020).

Chapter 2

1. Goldman Sachs Consumer and Investment Management Division (2020).
2. Merle and Telford (2020).
3. Winton (2018).
4. Dalio (2019).
5. PlanB (2020).
6. OKEx (2019).
7. Crescat Capital (2021).
8. Artemis Capital Management (2015).

Chapter 3

1. Mathiesen (2020).
2. Dalio (2019).
3. Dalio (2018).
4. Dalio (n.d.).
5. Federal Reserve Board Announces Updates to Secondary Market Corporate Credit Facility (SMCCF) (2020).
6. Bank for International Settlements (2020).

Chapter 4

1. PlanB (2019).
2. PlanB (2020).

Chapter 5

1. Cheng (2018).
2. Securities and Exchange Commission (2018).
3. Jones and Giorgianni (2020).
4. Saylor (2020).
5. Nakamoto (2009).
6. Ibid.

Chapter 6

1. Popper (2016).
2. Ibid.
3. Grauer and Udpdegrave (2021).
4. International Consortium of Investigative Journalists (2020).
5. Stanway (2018).
6. Blandin et al. (2021).
7. Rooney (2018).
8. Bloomberg (2018).
9. McAndrew (2017).
10. Kiel and Nguyen (2021).
11. Horowitz et al. (2020).
12. Wu (2012).
13. Manikandan and Price (2020).
14. Bitcoin Mining Map (2021).
15. de Best (2020).
16. China Blocks New Solar in 3 NW Regions amid Overcapacity Fears (2019).
17. Zhao (2019).

Chapter 7

1. Buterin (2020).
2. Buterin (2020).
3. Buterin (2013).
4. Cryptus (2019).
5. Bramblet (2020).
6. Blockchain on AWS - Enterprise Blockchain Made Real (2021).
7. Siegel (2020).
8. Buterin (n.d.).
9. Alyssa (2020).
10. Mark (2020).

Chapter 8

1. Santos-Alborna (2020).
2. Interest Expense on the Debt Outstanding (2021).
3. Evans (2019).
4. Pal and Velez (2021).

Conclusion

1. "Medical Cost Trend: Behind the Numbers 2021." (June 2020).

References

"Federal Reserve Board Announces Updates to Secondary Market Corporate Credit Facility (SMCCF), Which Will Begin Buying a Broad and Diversified Portfolio of Corporate Bonds to Support Market Liquidity and the Availability of Credit for Large Employers." June 15, 2020. Board of Governors of the Federal Reserve System. https://federalreserve.gov/newsevents/pressreleases/monetary20200615a.htm

"Interest Expense on the Debt Outstanding." *Treasury Direct.* 2021. https://treasurydirect.gov/govt/reports/ir/ir_expense.htm

2021. "Blockchain on AWS - Enterprise Blockchain Made Real." *Amazon Web Services*, Inc., https://aws.amazon.com/blockchain/

Alyssa, H. July 20, 2020. "This New Coding Language Could Help Unlock Bitcoin's Smart Contract Potential." *CoinDesk*, https://coindesk.com/this-new-coding-language-could-help-unlock-bitcoins-smart-contract-potential

Ammous, S. 2018. *The Bitcoin Standard: The Decentralized Alternative to Central Banking.* Hoboken, NJ: John Wiley & Sons.

Apolline, B., G. Pieters, Y. Wu, T. Eisermann, A. Dek, S. Taylor, and D. Njoki. 2021. *Global Cryptoasset Benchmarking Study*, 3rd ed. Cambridge, United Kingdom: Center for Alternative Finance.

Artemis Capital Management. October, 2015. "Volatility and the Allegory of the Prisoner's Dilemma." https://artemiscm.com/welcome#research

Bank for International Settlements. October 2020. *Central Bank Digital Currencies: Foundational Principles and Core Features.*

Benedict Evans. August 4, 2019. "In Praise of Failure." *ben-evans.com*, https://ben-evans.com/benedictevans/2016/4/28/winning-and-losing

Bloomberg. July 12, 2018. "More MBA Graduates Are Choosing Tech Jobs, and Silicon Valley Is Hiring." *Business Standard*, https://business-standard.com/article/education/mba-students-seek-sexy-tech-jobs-and-silicon-valley-is-hiring-118071201137_1.html#:~:text=Luckily%20for%20him%20and%20many,of%20finance%20and%20accounting%20firms

Bramblet, J. August 11, 2020. "Ultimate Guide to Blockchain in Insurance." *Accenture Insurance Blog*, https://insuranceblog.accenture.com/ultimate-guide-to-blockchain-in-insurance.

Buterin, V. 2013. "A Next-Generation Smart Contract and Decentralized Application Platform." ethereum.org, 2013. https://ethereum.org/en/whitepaper/

Buterin, V. Twitter Post. August 7, 2020. 6:12 PM. https://twitter.com/VitalikButerin/status/1291890093918052353

Buterin, V. Twitter Post. June 17, 2020. 6:01 AM. https://twitter.com/VitalikButerin/status/1273224124882657280

Buterin. (n.d). "A Next-Generation Smart Contract and Decentralized Application Platform."

Cambridge Bitcoin Electricity Consumption Index (CBECI). 2021. "Bitcoin Mining Map." https://cbeci.org/mining_map

Cheng, E. January 4, 2018. "Merrill Lynch Bans Its Clients, Advisors from Trading Bitcoin-Related Investments." *CNBC*, https://www.cnbc.com/2018/01/03/merrill-lynch-bans-its-clients-advisors-from-trading-bitcoin-related-investments-report-says.html

Crescat Capital. January 28, 2021. "Crescat Capital Quarterly Investor Letter Q4 2020." https://crescat.net/crescat-capital-quarterly-investor-letter-q4-2020/

Dalio, R. 2018. *Principles for Navigating Big Debt Crises*. Westport, CT: Bridgewater Associates.

Dalio, R. 2019. "Diversifying Well Is the Most Important Thing You Need to Do in Order to Invest Well." *LinkedIn*, https://linkedin.com/pulse/diversifying-well-most-important-thing-you-need-do-order-ray-dalio/

Dalio, R. July 17, 2019. "Paradigm Shifts." *LinkedIn*, https://linkedin.com/pulse/paradigm-shifts-ray-dalio

Dalio, R. n.d. "Paradigm Shifts."

Daly, L. 2020. "Average Credit Card Processing Fees and Costs in 2020: The Ascent." *The Motley Fool*, July 8, 2020. https://fool.com/the-ascent/research/average-credit-card-processing-fees-costs-america/#:~:text=The%20average%20credit%20card%20processing,assessment%20fees%2C%20and%20processing%20fees

de Best, R. January 13, 2021. "Bitcoin Trading Volume on Online Exchanges in Various Countries Worldwide in 2020." *Statista*, https://statista.com/statistics/1195753/bitcoin-trading-selected-countries/

Eustace Cryptus. "2017's ICO Boom Was The Bubble That Will Never Recover." *Bitcoinist.com*, August 9, 2019. https://bitcoinist.com/2017s-ico-boom-was-the-bubble-that-will-never-recover/

February 15, 2019. "China Blocks New Solar in 3 NW Regions amid Overcapacity Fears." *Reuters*, https://reuters.com/article/us-china-solarpower/china-blocks-new-solar-in-3-nw-regions-amid-overcapacity-fears-idUSKCN1Q404G

Goldman Sachs Consumer and Investment Management Division. May 27, 2020. "US Economic Outlook & Implications of Current Policies for Inflation, Gold and Bitcoin (15th in COVID-19 Series)." Investor Call Presentation.

Grauer, K., and H. Udpdegrave. 2021. *The 2021 Crypto Crime Report*. Chainalysis Inc.

Gromen, L., Interview with E. Townsend, and P. Ceresna. 2020. "Macro Voices." *Podcast Audio*, June 8, 2020, https://macrovoices.com/podcasts-collection/macrovoices-all-stars-podcasts/857-all-stars-108-luke-gromen-central-banks-on-steroids

Horowitz, J.M., R. Igielnik, and R. Kochhar. August 17, 2020. "Trends in U.S. Income and Wealth Inequality." *Pew Research Center's Social & Demographic Trends Project. Pew Research Center.* https://pewresearch.org/social-trends/2020/01/09/trends-in-income-and-wealth-inequality/

International Consortium of Investigative Journalists. December 22, 2020. "Global Banks Defy U.S. Crackdowns by Serving Oligarchs, Criminals and Terrorists." *ICIJ*, https://icij.org/investigations/fincen-files/global-banks-defy-u-s-crackdowns-by-serving-oligarchs-criminals-and-terrorists/

Jones, P., and L. Giorgianni. May 7, 2020. "The Great Monetary Inflation." *Market Outlook – Macro Perspective.*

June 2020. "Medical Cost Trend: Behind the Numbers 2021." *Price Waterhouse Cooper Health Research Institute.* https://pwc.com/us/en/industries/health-industries/library/behind-the-numbers.html.

Kaylani, M. 2019. "At Delhi's First Oxygen Bar, Breathe in 'Pure Air' for Rs 300." *The Indian Express*, November 18, 2019. https://indianexpress.com/article/lifestyle/health/at-delhis-first-oxygen-bar-breathe-in-pure-air-for-rs-300-6123330/

Kiel, P., and D. Nguyen. 2021. "Bailout Tracker." *ProPublica*, February 16, 2021. https://projects.propublica.org/bailout/list

Manikandan, A., and M. Price. September 29, 2020. "JPMorgan to Pay $920 Million for Manipulating Precious Metals, Treasury Market." *Reuters*, https://reuters.com/article/jp-morgan-spoofing-penalty/jpmorgan-to-pay-920-million-for-manipulating-precious-metals-treasury-market-idUSKBN26K325

Mark, K. November 2, 2020. "Global Plug-In Electric Car Sales September 2020: Massive Record." *InsideEVs*, https://insideevs.com/news/451774/global-plugin-electric-car-sales-september-2020/

Mathiesen, K. "Why Licence Plate Bans Don't Cut Smog." The Guardian. Guardian News and Media, March 20, 2014. https://theguardian.com/cities/2014/mar/20/licence-plate-driving-bans-paris-ineffective-air-pollution

Mauldin, J., and L. Hunt. October 16, 2020. "Caught in a Debt Trap." *Advisor Perspectives*, https://advisorperspectives.com/commentaries/2020/10/16/caught-in-a-debt-trap

McAndrew, C. 2017. *The Art Market 2017.* Art Basel & UBS.

Merle, R., and T. Telford. July 24, 2020. "Goldman Sachs Reaches $3.9 Billion Settlement in 1MDB Scandal." *The Washington Post. WP Company* https://washingtonpost.com/business/2020/07/24/goldman-sachs-1mdb-scandal-settlement/

Nakamoto, S. February 11, 2009. "Bitcoin Open Source Implementation of P2P Currency." *P2P Foundation* (discussion board), http://p2pfoundation.ning.com/forum/topics/bitcoin-open-source.

OKEx. August 16, 2019. "Sharpe Ratio and Crypto." *Medium*, https://medium.com/okex-blog/sharpe-ratio-and-crypto-10a1c083c63b#:~:text=Bitcoin%20has%20been%20giving%20a,back%20to%20around%201.3%20level

Pal, R., and S. Velez. January 20, 2021. "The Inconvenient Truth About Cryptocurrencies." *Macro Insiders*.

PlanB. April 27, 2020. "Bitcoin Stock-to-Flow Cross Asset Model. *Medium*, https://medium.com/@100trillionUSD/bitcoin-stock-to-flow-cross-asset-model-50d260feed12

PlanB. January 17, 2020. "Efficient Market Hypothesis and Bitcoin Stock-to-Flow Model." *Medium*, https://medium.com/@100trillionUSD/efficient-market-hypothesis-and-bitcoin-stock-to-flow-model-db17f40e6107.

PlanB. March 22, 2019. "Modeling Bitcoin Value with Scarcity." *Medium*, https://medium.com/@100trillionUSD/modeling-bitcoins-value-with-scarcity-91fa0fc03e25

Popper, N. 2016. *Digital Gold: Bitcoin and the Inside Story of the Misfits and Millionaires Trying to Reinvent Money.* New York, NY: Harper.

Reuters. 2020. "Twitter Post." September 10, 2020, 5:10 AM. https://twitter.com/reuters/status/1304014254035677186?lang=en

Rooney. K. June 6, 2018. "An Old Alcoa Plant in Upstate New York Is Going to Be Converted into One of the World's Largest Bitcoin Mining Centers." *CNBC*, https://cnbc.com/2018/06/05/bitcoin-miner-revamps-alcoas-aluminum-factory.html.

Santos-Alborna, A. July 1, 2020. "The Anti-Fragile Portfolio." *SeekingAlpha*, https://seekingalpha.com/article/4356505-anti-fragile-portfolio

Saylor, M., interview with P. Pysh. December 22, 2020. "The Investor's Podcast (BTC005)." *Podcast Audio*, https://theinvestorspodcast.com/bitcoin-fundamentals/btc005-bitcoin-michael-saylor-a-masterclass-in-economic-calculation/

Securities and Exchange Commission. 2018. *Order Setting Aside Action by Delegated Authority and Disapproving a Proposed Rule Change, as Modified by Amendments No. 1 and 2, to List and Trade Shares of the Winklevoss Bitcoin Trust.*

Siegel, D. December 17, 2020. "The DAO Attack: Understanding What Happened." *CoinDesk*, https://coindesk.com/understanding-dao-hack-journalists.

Stanway, D. August 30, 2018. "Dam Nation: Big State Projects Spared in China's Hydro Crackdown." *Reuters*, https://reuters.com/article/us-china-hydropower/dam-nation-big-state-projects-spared-in-chinas-hydro-crackdown-idUSKCN1LF2RG

Winton, A. September 18, 2018. "Get A Horse! America's Skepticism Toward the First Automobiles." *The Saturday Evening Post*. https://saturdayeveningpost.com/2017/01/get-horse-americas-skepticism-toward-first-automobiles/

Wu, T. 2012. *The Master Switch: The Rise and Fall of Information Empires*. London: Atlantic.

Zhao, W. 2019. "China's New Policy Isn't An Automatic Bitcoin Mining Ban— Here's Why." *CoinDesk*, April 11, 2019. https://coindesk.com/chinas-new-policy-isnt-an-automatic-bitcoin-mining-ban-heres-why

About the Author

Ariel Santos-Alborna is an investor, writer, and entrepreneur. Ariel has published over 40 articles specializing in finance and macroeconomic investments with a focus on secular trends as a contributor on seekin galpha.com. In addition to his investment recommendations, Ariel frequently provides commentary on the social, political, and economic implications of global central bank policy and blockchain technology. Ariel began investing in Bitcoin in late 2018 and published his first buy recommendation, "Buy the Dip on Bitcoin," in July 2019. He began his own research service, ASA Macro, through the Seeking Alpha Marketplace in 2020. Ariel graduated from the United States Military Academy at West Point in 2017 with a Bachelor of Science in International Relations and Political Economics. He served over four years as a U.S. Army Infantry officer.

Index

OTHER TITLES IN THE FINANCE AND FINANCIAL MANAGEMENT COLLECTION

John Doukas, Old Dominion University, Editor

- *Understanding the Financial Industry Through Linguistics* by Richard C. Robinson
- *Sustainable Finance and Impact Investing* by Alan S. Gutterman
- *The Non-Timing Trading System* by George O. Head
- *Small Business Finance and Valuation* by Rick Nason and Dan Nordqvist
- *Finance for Non-Finance Executives* by Anurag Singal
- *Blockchain Hurricane* by Kate Baucherel
- *Risk Management for Nonprofit Organizations* by Rick Nason and Omer Livvarcin
- *Conservative Options Trading* by Michael C. Thomsett
- *Understanding Behavioral BIA$* by Daniel C. Krawczyk and George H. Baxter
- *Valuation of Indian Life Insurance Companies* by Prasanna Rajesh
- *Understanding Momentum in Investment Technical Analysis* by Michael C. Thomsett
- *Trade Credit and Financing Instruments* by Lucia Gibilaro
- *Trade Credit and Risk Management* by Lucia Gibilaro
- *Mastering Options* by PhilipCooper
- *Understanding Cryptocurrencies* by Arvind Matharu
- *The Art and Science of Financial Modeling* by Anurag Singal

Concise and Applied Business Books

The Collection listed above is one of 30 business subject collections that Business Expert Press has grown to make BEP a premiere publisher of print and digital books. Our concise and applied books are for...

- Professionals and Practitioners
- Faculty who adopt our books for courses
- Librarians who know that BEP's Digital Libraries are a unique way to offer students ebooks to download, not restricted with any digital rights management
- Executive Training Course Leaders
- Business Seminar Organizers

Business Expert Press books are for anyone who needs to dig deeper on business ideas, goals, and solutions to everyday problems. Whether one print book, one ebook, or buying a digital library of 110 ebooks, we remain the affordable and smart way to be business smart. For more information, please visit www.businessexpertpress.com, or contact sales@businessexpertpress.com.

www.ingramcontent.com/pod-product-compliance
Lightning Source LLC
Chambersburg PA
CBHW061324220326
41599CB00026B/5030